WITHDRAWN

D1071392

BUCKNELL REVIEW

Literature and Ideology

STATEMENT OF POLICY

Bucknell Review is a scholarly interdisciplinary journal. Each issue is devoted to a major theme or movement in the humanities or sciences, or to two or three closely related topics. The editors invite heterodox, orthodox, and speculative ideas and welcome manuscripts from any enterprising scholar in the humanities and sciences.

BUCKNELL REVIEW
A Scholarly Journal of Letters, Arts and Sciences

Editor
HARRY R. GARVIN

Associate Editor
JAMES M. HEATH

Editorial Board
PATRICK BRADY
JAMES M. HEATH
STEVEN MAILLOUX
MICHAEL D. PAYNE
JOHN WHEATCROFT

Assistants to the Editor
DOROTHY L. BAUMWOLL
JANE S. BRUMBACH

Contributors should send manuscripts with a self-addressed stamped envelope to the Editor, Bucknell University, Lewisburg, Pennsylvania 17837.

BUCKNELL REVIEW

Literature and Ideology

Edited by
HARRY R. GARVIN

Special Associate Editor This Issue
JAMES M. HEATH

LEWISBURG
BUCKNELL UNIVERSITY PRESS
LONDON AND TORONTO: ASSOCIATED UNIVERSITY PRESSES

© 1982 by Associated University Presses, Inc.

Associated University Presses, Inc.
4 Cornwall Drive
East Brunswick, N.J. 08816

Associated University Presses Ltd
27 Chancery Lane
London WC2A, 1NF England

Associated University Presses
Toronto M5E 1A7, Canada

Library of Congress Cataloging in Publication Data
Main entry under title:

Literature and ideology.

    (Bucknell review; v. 27, no. 1)
    Includes bibliographical references.
    Contents: Introduction / James M. Heath—
George Orwell, the novelist displaced / David
M. Zehr—The poem that failed: the Auden
group's retreat from political verse / Thomas
Mallon—[etc.]
    1. Literature and society—Addresses,
essays, lectures. I. Garvin, Harry Raphael,
1917– . II. Heath, James M. III. Series.
AP2.B887   vol. 27, no. 1   051s [809]   81-69441
[PN51]   AACR2
ISBN 0-8387-5049-4

(Volume XXVII, Number 1)

Printed in the United States of America

83-01742

Contents

Notes on Contributors

ANGELIKA BAMMER: Teaches at the University of Wisconsin–Madison. Papers and articles on Marxist-feminist criticism, the relations between feminist scholarship and nonestablishment presses, and women's use of the utopian genre. Special interests: an ideological critique of traditional genre categories, women's diaries as a subversive literary form. Current project: the utopian impulse in contemporary feminist writings.

RONALD L. BOGUE: Teaches at the University of Georgia. Has published several essays on Pope, Barthes, and Robbe-Grillet. Major interests: eighteenth-century aesthetics, postmodernism, and contemporary critical theory.

DIANE GRIFFIN CROWDER: Teaches at Cornell College. Research interests include literary theory and contemporary French fiction. Many papers on semiotics, feminist criticism, Colette, and pedagogy. Currently preparing a book on semiotics and feminist criticism.

CAROLYN A. DURHAM: Teaches at the College of Wooster. Main professional interests: twentieth-century French novel and feminist literary criticism. Publications on language as culture, the French New Novel, the romanesque art of Raymond Roussel. Research in progress: the mother-daughter relationship in the eighteenth-century feminocentric novel, particularly Diderot's *La Religieuse* and Bernardin's *Paul et Virginie*.

JAMES H. KAVANAGH: Teaches at Princeton University. Has published essays on Marxist critical theory, modern fiction, and contemporary film. Serves as an advisory editor for *Praxis*, and in the editorial collective of *Social Text*.

7

THOMAS MALLON: Teaches at Vassar College. Publications on Oscar Wilde, Yeats, Sassoon, Joan Didion, numerous reviews, book-length study of Edmund Blunden. Current projects: a book about diarists; literary biography; twentieth-century novel.

BROOK THOMAS: Teaches at the University of Hawaii, Manoa. Has published numerous essays on James Joyce, Twain, Melville, Hawthorne, and critical theory. His present research compares textual and interpretive strategies in nineteenth-century American literature and law.

DAVID M. ZEHR: Teaches at the University of Alabama at Birmingham. Publications on Ernest Hemingway and Joyce. Work in progress: a book on George Orwell.

STEPHEN ZELNICK: Teaches at Temple University. The national organizer for the Marxist Literary Group and the editor of *Mediations*, the MLG newsletter. Publications in Marxist literary criticism; essays on Fitzgerald, Conrad, and educational reform theory; a book on the novel and history.

Introduction

Literary figures create worlds, and the worlds they create reflect in complex ways the external worlds they experience. These author-created worlds also interact in complex ways with those worlds which readers inhabit and conceptualize. Such created worlds comprise not only physical phenomena but, more important, human behavior. Authors write into their work and readers read into it societies that differ variously from familiar ones. But beyond these representations lie still others of a less easily recognized kind: structures of assumed values and traditions, scientific explanations, philosophic conceptions of ultimate reality. The study of ideology in literature involves an analysis of both the reflection of all such realities in literary works and their perception by others.

This issue of *Bucknell Review* considers questions of contemporary significance that arise in the study of ideology in literature. The editors approach the topic from three viewpoints. The first section examines certain writers as they incorporate in their work ideological content in some more or less conscious form. The second section illustrates the approach of critics attempting to understand literary works while at the same time remaining aware that, as readers and critics, they are subject to ideological claims and pressures of a different order. The final section takes up the particular case of women, who, whether as writers, as critic-readers, or as actors in the world, face the problems of ideology from a perspective that differs significantly from and often conflicts with that of the male writer-reader-critic-actor.

It is not possible to disentangle entirely these three threads; all, really, emerge from the same ball of yarn. But in observing the consequences of following different threads in the three sections, no scholar or reader can long remain aloof from self-involvement and self-criticism. An investigation of the effect of real or imagined or theorized worlds on writers and critics reveals a fundamental complexity in literature.

No past or contemporary definitions of the term *ideology* en-

tirely satisfy our purpose in this issue. Whether referring to
something that characterizes a society, a critic, or a class—or
even to "the truth"—ideology says something important about
how conceptions of the world form an essential component of
literature and its interpretation. The critics in this issue use the
term in their own fashion; the differences are themselves instructive.

The first approach, investigating ways in which authors represent political and social issues in their work and in consequence reevaluate their function as authors, characterizes the
two papers of the first section. Zehr and Mallon, writing on
Orwell and the "Auden group," discuss issues that will arise in
more pointed and theoretical forms in the succeeding sections:
the relevance to societal and literary concerns of Marxist theory
and practice, the responsibilities of a literary figure in and to a
sociopolitical context, the conflicts in which being a writer involves an actor and critic of the society and its literature. Orwell
turns from a leftist or liberal stance into a disillusioned pessimism, about both the world and the role of the novel in that
world. The poets associated with Auden, too, lose their idealism
and political enthusiasm but gain in poetic richness.

The papers of the second group isolate certain features that
help to characterize the contemporary critic who approaches
literature, of both modern and earlier times, from the perspective of ideology. Such a critic attempts not merely to disentangle from a work of literature those features which make it
"ideological," but also to examine how earlier critics have mis-
read authors by misrepresenting or, more often, ignoring
ideology. All four critics, in adopting or at least considering a
Marxist approach to their topics, are instructive by their varied
applications and conceptions of that approach.

Thomas attempts to discover which character in *Billy Budd*
best represents the viewpoint, or the contradictions within the
viewpoint, of Melville. His focus on Captain Vere and the contradictions within that character allows him to relate questions
of authority and innocence in the novel to sociopolitical questions of Melville's day, to the criticism of Melville, and to Melville's doubts about his own role as writer. Zelnick develops a
similar analysis of *Robinson Crusoe,* showing how the protagonist
becomes a prototype of the capitalist.in the ideology that is
beginning to emerge in Defoe's time and to affect the development of the novel as a genre. Kavanagh's goal is even

more ambitious: to demonstrate that the concept of the aesthetic is itself a construct and a matter of ideology. While discussing how the literary "text" is produced as the artifact of a particular era and ideology, he points to the workers' production of a dramatic text in *A Midsummer Night's Dream* as one kind of illustrative source of the modern concept. Bogue examines the critiques of popular culture developed by Roland Barthes and Jean Baudrillard. By relating Barthes's analysis of a pasta advertisement as a dual message with symbolic and nonsymbolic components to Baudrillard's opposition of exchange value and usage value, he finds fruitful approaches to an understanding of ideology.

Women provide the focus for the third group of papers: as critics, as feminists, as Marxist revolutionaries and theorists. The authors consider how women are affected in their lives and work by the ideologies and realities of their societies, while the works of literature and criticism they produce are gently or forcibly ignored or suppressed—ironically, often in the name of the "higher interests" of their societies and the theories on which they are based. Looking at the work of women writer-actors in recent revolutionary contexts, Bammer is concerned with how such women reconcile their personal Marxism and the patriarchal societal expectations of more traditional Marxism. Crowder's semiotic approach to the ideological aspects of the portrayal of women in literature focuses on the signs that point to the signified "woman." Analyzing a Garden of Eden passage in a work of Monique Wittig, she shows how a different use of signs can make that most patriarchal of myths a feminist one. Finally, Durham examines the work of the feminist critic Claudine Herrmann and her attempts to go beyond or outside latter-day ideology.

The editors hope that the complexities in the interrelationship of literature and ideology that these papers reveal will lead to increased interest in and further exploration of this vital issue in contemporary literature and criticism.

James M. Heath
Associate Editor

BUCKNELL REVIEW

Literature and Ideology

Writers and
Ideology

George Orwell: The Novelist Displaced

David M. Zehr
University of Alabama

I

GEORGE Orwell's development from a relatively conventional novelist with a belletristic view of his art into a politicized novelist and man of letters whose work helped to shape the mood of the Cold War period was a painful intellectual journey made at considerable cost to his imaginative and cultural confidence—a journey that sheds critical light for us on the dilemmas and pressures Orwell faced during a period of social and political upheaval, and one that further clarifies the perennially uneasy, problematic relationship between imagination and conscience. Between 1933 and 1939 Orwell published seven books: four novels (*Burmese Days, A Clergyman's Daughter, Keep the Aspidistra Flying,* and *Coming Up for Air*), two autobiographical memoirs (*Down and Out in Paris and London* and *Homage to Catalonia*, both works of art, rendered with varying degrees of aesthetic detachment), and one documentary (*The Road to Wigan Pier*). Despite the discipline and commitment this production of seven works in seven years demonstrates, and the fact that he was writing with increasing authority and confidence by 1939, he was to write only two more books during the following decade—*Animal Farm* and *Nineteen Eighty-four*, the two works that are such radical departures in form from his previous work and that so powerfully dramatize the mounting sense of political urgency and cultural anxiety he felt during the 1940s. To see this dramatic change in the direction of his literary career simply as the result of his evolution into a political writer who came to recognize the inadequacy of realistic

17

fiction, as Alex Zwerdling suggests,[1] is to ignore the deeper intellectual and emotional dynamics that so traumatically affected Orwell's imagination. The political commitment he made in 1936 (when he declared himself "*against* totalitarianism and *for* democratic socialism, as I understand it") did not transform him into a polemicist or an ideologue, or lead him to a quest for radical new forms; on the contrary, his emergent political consciousness would seem to be at least partly responsible for the increased air of confidence, authority, and vitality in his last two works of the 1930s, *Homage to Catalonia* (1938) and *Coming Up for Air* (1939)—both of which are highly political, and yet still relatively conventional works of art. And although Orwell did turn away from the mainstream of the English novel during the 1940s, he continued to insist upon the cultural importance of maintaining an independent, liberal tradition of the English novel, being convinced that the survival of such a tradition was complexly linked with the survival of English liberal-bourgeois culture itself. But during the 1940s he became convinced that the liberal-bourgeois tradition with which he identified himself and his vocation was undergoing cataclysmic, possibly irreversible, fragmentation, and as he became increasingly apocalyptic his faith in the tradition of the novel was severely undercut.

What I would like to suggest is that about 1939 or 1940 Orwell experienced a profound crisis of cultural faith that deeply disrupted his imaginative stability, and that it was the personal and cultural anxiety that resulted from this crisis, and not simply a distrust in the form of the novel, that led to the profound shift in the direction and complexion of his literary career during the 1940s—a shift, I believe, that Orwell was not entirely comfortable with. While other writers have long noted that there exists a break or a shift in the direction of Orwell's career around 1940, I would like to demonstrate that he experienced a crisis of imaginative and cultural confidence that had profound reverberations upon his work, and to suggest that this crisis can in part be understood by examining Orwell's idiosyncratic, rather old-fashioned, conception of the novel and his view of the cultural role of the novelist.

II

When Orwell committed himself to a literary career at the age of twenty-four his aesthetic attitudes were for the most part unoriginal and old-fashioned, generally reflecting his Etonian background and his reading of Victorian and Edwardian writers. In both his early reviews and letters he demonstrated an essentially belletristic view of art; in his 1930 review of J. B. Priestley's *Angel Pavement* he suggested that "a novelist is not required to have good intentions but to convey beauty."[2] And in a 1933 letter he set forth his sense of what a novel should do: "I should say that it sets out first . . . to display or create character, secondly to make a kind of pattern or design which any good story contains, and thirdly, if the novelist is up to it, to produce *good writing,* which can exist almost as it were in vacuo and independent of subject" (1:126). This curiously aesthetic response (notably lacking any political, social, or moral purpose) reveals Orwell's conventionalized conception of the novel in his early years, and the degree to which he had been uninfluenced by the modernist movement (not to mention the growing interest in politics of his contemporaries). He was certainly sensitive to the achievements of Lawrence and Joyce (he admired both, but did not read them until the early 1930s), yet throughout the 1930s he continued to identify as his masters those writers of the English naturalist tradition—Hardy, Gissing, Wells, Maugham, Galsworthy—whom he identified (along with Dickens) as writing at the center of an English cultural tradition. And it is indicative of the degree to which he was unaffected by the self-consciousness of the modernist movement that he saw the novel as an expansive form that, unlike poetry or the short story, provided the writer with lots of "elbow room." In 1936 (significantly, the year of his political conversion) he declared his belief that the novelist "is primarily a storyteller," and four years later he said that "the modern writer who has influenced me most is Somerset Maugham, whom I admire immensely for his power of telling a story straightforwardly and without frills" (1:253; 2:24). In other words, at the same time that Orwell was developing a more complex moral and social consciousness, his conception of the novel remained static; he continued to see the novel according to the conventions and norms that characterized his early reading rather than as a form that might be newly forged in order to meet the needs of one's own vision and experience (as Lawrence, Joyce, and Virginia Woolf had done, and as many of his contemporaries, such as Waugh and Isherwood, were doing). And we shall be able to see that this conceptual limitation became a key factor in his shift away from the form of the novel after 1939. But first we need to understand his perception of the novelist's situation during the last four years of the thirties.

Despite his lack of interest in innovation or theory, after 1936 Orwell did become increasingly concerned about the status of the novel, a devaluation of which he feared would undercut his power as a writer by narrowing his audience. In a 1936 essay, "In Defense of the Novel," he says: "To admit you like novels is nowadays almost equivalent to admitting that you have a hankering after coconut ice or prefer Rupert Brooke to Gerard Manley Hopkins" (1:250–51). He suggests that this lapse in fashion is the result of the "disgusting tripe that is written by the blurb reviewers," which he felt was erasing standards and blurring gradations. But he ignores the fact that the political consciousness of the 1930s had led to a growing demand for the documentary, the essay, and the expressly political novel. In addition, poetry, in the hands of such fashionably political writers as Auden, Spender, and Day Lewis, had come to enjoy a prestige that further contributed to the novel's being seen as an escapist, bourgeois form. By 1939 Orwell had not altered his evaluation of the status of the novel, but he had revised his diagnosis: he looked back over the decade and announced, curiously, that he found "practically no fiction of any value at all"—because, he said, "the mental climate was increasingly against it" (1:518). Orwell's perception of this "mental climate" is necessary to an understanding of his evolving attitude toward the situation of the writer in the late 1930s, and to his mounting pessimism. First, he believed that following the rise of Hitler in 1933 growing feelings of cultural anxiety over the prospects of war had created an air of tension and unease that unsettled the imaginative stability of the writer and altered the mood and expectations of the reading public. Second, and more important, Orwell identified this "mental climate" with the politicization of literature by an intelligentsia he felt had, in general, embraced an orthodoxy of leftist politics, and he saw this fascination with orthodoxy as exerting a serious threat to the survival of an intellectually independent, vital tradition of the novel. Orwell certainly came to see himself as a political writer, but he was also passionately opposed to the Communist Party, at odds with the mainstream of English leftist politics, and openly hostile to many English writers who had become fashionably political.[3] In fact, Orwell's insistent rejection of the rigidities of political orthodoxy repeatedly set him at odds with the literary left. The facts that Victor Gollancz (the founder of the Left Book Club, and the publisher of Orwell's first five books) felt compelled to add a critical foreword to *The Road to Wigan Pier* (1937) in order to take issue with Orwell's idiosyncratic socialism, and then refused to publish *Homage to Catalonia* because of what he saw as its heretical political point of view (specifically, Orwell's attack on the effects of Russian intervention in Spain), suggest the degree of Orwell's alienation from the mainstream of England's literary left at the time, and the origin of many of his anxieties about the effect of politics on literature.

One of the principal factors that disturbed Orwell about the literary left was what he saw as its devaluation of imaginative literature—specifically, the repeated insistence that literature should be primarily utilitarian, that it should be a servant of the cause. There was certainly, as a result of the heightened political consciousness of the time, a growing interest in the factual, in the documentary, in what could be examined beneath the writer's noninterpretive (although sometimes myopic) microscope. For example, the Left Book Club generally preferred overtly political or documentary works to fiction, but when it offered Belfrage's novel *Promised Land,* Gollancz defended the choice by saying, "it is in fictional form, but the disguise is a very thin one."[4] And in 1939 Stephen Spender announced in a journal named *Fact* that the magazine would no longer review novels "unless they derive from a basis of factual material such as might form a number of *Fact* itself."[5] Perhaps the extreme of this point of view is demonstrated by the Marxist writer Edward Upward, who declared that unless the writer "has in everyday life taken the side of the workers, he cannot, no matter how talented he may be, write a good book, cannot tell the truth about reality," and that as a result his writing will become "increasingly false, worthless as literature."[6] Orwell was convinced that a serious writer could not ignore the pressing political issues of his time—and that if he did so he was either "a footler or a plain idiot"—but he also believed that the subjugation of art to political dogma would mean the crippling of the writer and the death of literature. He repeatedly insisted that adherence to a particular ideology (what he called the "smelly little orthodoxies") would limit the free range of the writer's mind and consciousness (and conscience) and impose false patterns of character and construction upon art, turning literature into

a facile cog of a machine state or of a particular party (which is
precisely what does happen to literature in the world of *Nineteen Eighty-four,* where Julia operates a novel-writing machine).
A telling example of this concern is Orwell's response to *The
Calf of Paper,* by Sholem Asch, a German novel that depicts
conditions in 1936 Germany—inflation, starvation, anti-
Semitism, the operations of Hitler and his gang. Orwell revealed his essential concerns by taking issue with the work aes-
thetically. After admitting that the work does some service by
providing the reading public with historically and politically
crucial information, he criticizes it by saying that "there is not a
single scene, character or piece of dialogue which is there because it has forced itself upon him as material *ought* to force
itself upon a novelist" (1:247). Orwell did not see the writer's
political commitment as necessarily in opposition to his integrity as an artist, but he became increasingly convinced during
the 1930s that aesthetic integrity had often been subsumed by
dogma and polemic, resulting in the writing of historical-
political documents only thinly and awkwardly disguised as
novels. And Orwell saw this blurring of ideology and literature
as representing a gradual erosion of the power of literature and
of the independence of the novelist—and a significant step toward the world of Oceania.

Orwell's second major indictment of the literary left was his
insistence that despite the fashionable cult of the proletariat
"literature has moved no nearer to the masses" (1:512). Indeed,
he maintained that leftist writers, infatuated with power and
orthodoxy, had become culturally deracinated—severed from
the social and moral roots of a common English culture—and
that as a result there was in their writing "less room . . . for the
ordinary man than at any time during the past two centuries"
(1:500). His rancor toward fashionable, elitist politics is further
reflected by his suggestion that "Auden and Spender are somewhat farther from being popular writers than Joyce and Eliot,
let alone Lawrence" (1:512). Although Orwell's baiting of leftist
writers and intellectuals was often bitter and irrational (and
requires further psychological study),[7] he was nevertheless
genuinely concerned with preserving an independent, moral
tradition of the English novel, one that would reflect common
English culture and embody what he saw as traditional, normative values. And many critics have ignored the degree to which
this fundamentally conservative notion became complexly in-
terwoven with his conception of being a political writer.

In 1938 Orwell declared: "I am a writer. The impulse of every writer is to 'keep out of politics.' What he wants is to be left alone so that he can go on writing books in peace. But unfortunately it is becoming obvious that this ideal is no more practicable than that of the petty shop-keeper who hopes to preserve his independence in the teeth of the chain-store" (1:336). Despite this reluctant acceptance of political responsibility, Orwell's politics and his view of the writer's political role tended to be more characteristic of an English nineteenth-century liberal than of a 1930s radical. He personally interpreted the term *political* in its broadest sense—to include the writer's social vision and moral conscience. In his essay on Dickens he says that "every writer, especially every novelist, *has* a 'message,' whether he admits it or not, and the minutest details of his work are influenced by it. All art is propaganda. . . . On the other hand, not all propaganda is art" (1:448). In other words, Orwell's conception of being a political writer involved a belief in the novelist as a central social intelligence, charged with the responsibility of awakening and educating his readers to the urgent issues and problems of the day, without forsaking the integrity of his art and without accepting the dogma of a political ideology—and it was precisely to such a liberal, nineteenth-century ideal that he committed himself in the last years of the thirties.

Orwell's desire to transform the novelist back into a central social intelligence and to reintegrate the novel within the mainstream of English cultural life led him to support a revival of the novel as a serious form that would speak to a common-culture audience with the moral authority of shared experience and a common background—which is what he believed the Victorian and Edwardian novel had been able to do. While his first four books depict characters either living on the fringes of society or leading psychologically alienated lives, his fourth book, *Keep the Aspidistra Flying* (1936), concludes with Gordon Comstock's abandonment of his tepid revolt against society and with his reintegration into a normative English community. This novel not only marked the end of Orwell's own sense of social displacement, it also defined for him a new, more conservative, attitude toward what kind of novel it was important to write. When he reviewed Cyril Connolly's first novel, *The Rock Pool* (1936), which dramatizes English expatriates living the bohemian life in Paris, Orwell betrayed his biases by ignoring the aesthetic success or failure of the book and insisting that

"even to want to write about so-called artists who spend on
sodomy what they have gained by sponging betrays a kind of
spiritual inadequacy" (1:226). He believed that such literature
as Connolly's was perpetuating the schism between the literary
intelligentsia and a broad, common-culture audience, and thus
further contributing to the isolation, or marooning, of the
novelist. (Nevertheless, this reaction also displays Orwell's capacity for petulance and overreaction.) In a review dated the
same year he elaborates on this plea for normality in English
fiction, and his distrust of the alien, fringe life:

> English fiction on its highest levels is for the most part written by
> literary gents about literary gents for literary gents; on its lower
> levels it is generally the most putrid "escape" stuff—old maids' fan-
> tasies about Ian Hay male virgins, or little fat men's visions of them-
> selves as Chicago gangsters. Books about ordinary people behaving
> in an ordinary manner are extremely rare, because they can only be
> written by someone who is capable of standing inside and outside
> the ordinary man, as Joyce for instance stands inside and outside
> Bloom; but this involves admitting that you yourself *are* an ordinary
> person nine-tenths of the time, which is exactly what no intellectual
> ever wants to do. [1:230]

It was precisely such a fictional mode that Orwell set out to
write in his remarkably effective last work of the decade, *Coming Up for Air*—a broadly political novel that nevertheless cele-
brates the normative values of an ordinary, lower-middle-class
insurance salesman who has retained what Winston Smith calls
his "ancestral memory" amidst a time of tumultuous political
and cultural change. And because he has retained his culturally
rooted values and a memory of a less-fragmented communal
past, Orwell suggests that he is able to judge the social-political
crisis before him in 1938 with greater acuity, restraint, and
common sense than either the intellectuals or the ideologues.
Thus this is a political novel in the broadest sense, but it is also a
confident assertion of belief in the power of traditional, realistic
fiction to reach, and affect, a broad, common-culture audience.

Orwell's last major essay of the decade—"Inside the Whale"
(1939)—further develops what he had set out to accomplish in
Coming Up for Air, but it also provides a significant insight into
the conflict he was feeling between his own mounting militancy
and his continuing commitment to the value and function of a
nonideological, normative literature. Responding in this essay
to Henry Miller's *Tropic of Cancer*, he is both repelled and fas-

cinated by Miller's political passivity: he sees his passivity as an implicit acceptance of Hitler, Mussolini, Stalin, concentration camps, purges, etc., but he is attracted to him because he does not see him as an escapist—he describes Miller as fiddling while Rome burns, but fiddling with his face toward the flames. And he insists that this attitude accomplishes an important literary end: "precisely because, in one sense, he is passive to experience, Miller is able to get nearer to the ordinary man than is possible to more purposive writers" (1:500). He maintains that Miller's book records and dramatizes the authenticity of ordinary human experience, and thereby helps to preserve the value of the individual and the validity of subjective experience—values Orwell feared were being gradually undermined by a growing totalitarian habit of mind (which he saw both on the right and on the left). Thus, while he is unable to agree with or to accept Miller's political stance, he asserts that a fictional voice like his—"a voice from the crowd, from the underling, from the third-class carriage, from the ordinary, non-political, non-moral, passive man"—helps to preserve the idea and the experience of the autonomous individual, and to further deter the subversion of a liberal, individualistic society by power politics. Shortly before Orwell completed "Inside the Whale" Hitler marched into Poland, and for a complex of public and private reasons Orwell would not develop further the imaginative and cultural ideas he set forth in this essay and in *Coming Up for Air*. And it is at this point, at the height of his confidence, that he experienced a crisis of faith which profoundly altered his career.

Although he wrote only two more books after *Coming Up for Air*—both explicitly political, and both significant departures in form from his previous work—Orwell does not seem to have made any conscious decision to abandon the form of the novel in favor of more direct forms of expression, i.e., the essay, the pamphlet, or political fiction, which became his dominant mediums during the 1940s. In fact, during the years 1939 and 1940 he reaffirmed his continuing belief in the relevance and viability of the novel in a time of public crisis by planning a three-volume saga, tentatively titled "The English People." This work might have demonstrated the vitality and resiliency of Orwell's liberal concept of the novel by unifying his political militancy and his commitment to English common culture within a traditional fictive framework. Whether the work was too ambitious for him, or whether he was simply unable to synthesize at this traumatic point in time his imagination and conscience, is difficult to say, but he never got beyond the planning stages of his saga, and this would appear to be the first casualty of Orwell's crisis of confidence.[8]

III

The outbreak of war in September 1939 brought to a head Orwell's feelings of personal and cultural anxiety, and there now appeared in his writing a sharply accelerating tone of pessimism and near hysteria: "The literature of liberalism is coming to an end and the literature of totalitarianism has not yet appeared and is barely imaginable. As for the writer, he is sitting on a melting iceberg; he is merely an anachronism, a hangover from the bourgeois age, as surely doomed as the hippopotamus" (1:525–26). Although he continued to refer to his projected saga through the spring of 1940, his fears of cultural apocalypse gradually overwhelmed him, convincing him that both he and his culture had become dislocated from history. And this belief seems to have directly, and profoundly, disrupted the stability of his imagination: in 1941 he told the readers of *Partisan Review,* "Only the mentally dead are capable of sitting down and writing novels while this nightmare is going on. The conditions that made it possible for Joyce and Lawrence to do their best work during the war of 1914–18 (i.e., the consciousness that presently the world would be sane again) no longer exist. There is such a doubt about the continuity of civilization as can hardly have existed for hundreds of years" (2:54). Lawrence of course had had his own doubts about the sanity of his society and its ability to survive after the Great War, but, unlike Lawrence, Orwell seems to have been almost imaginatively crippled. His letters and essays reveal an increasingly strained, almost tortured, tone as he began to convert his own anxieties into ostensibly public evaluations. He was convinced that England as he knew it, a liberal-bourgeois tradition with which he identified his values, world view, sensibility, *and vocation,* was in the process of being radically displaced. As a result he came to feel that the kind of relationship that must exist between a novelist and his society (a familiar world of common experience and shared assumptions), the kind of relationship upon which he had predicated his attempt to renovate the novel in his own way during the final years of the thirties, no longer existed between himself and the ideological, polarized world of the 1940s. It is important to remember two things at this point: first, part of Orwell's painful malaise stemmed from the fact that he continued to see himself as a novelist, and not just as a man of letters; second, he tried to validate his own imaginative crisis by identifying it as part of a public crisis.

Orwell was by no means inactive during the forties. He worked for the BBC during the early years of the war, and then became literary editor of the left-wing *Tribune;* he also wrote a prodigious number of reviews, articles, and essays, as a glance at *The Collected Essays, Journalism, and Letters of George Orwell* will confirm (three of the four volumes are devoted to the 1940s). But despite the vigor of his pieces on popular culture and the acuity of many of his social and political essays, he continued to diagnose his own estrangement from fiction as symptomatic of a broader imaginative malaise. He complained that he was living in a time when "any sort of *joy* in writing, any such notion as telling a story for the purpose of pure entertainment, has . . . become impossible" (2:165). And when he reviewed Graham Greene's *The Heart of the Matter* in 1948 (indicating that this mood of crisis persisted long after the war) he concluded an otherwise negative response by saying that nevertheless "in post-war England it is a remarkable feat for a novelist to write a novel at all" (4:443). While the war years were certainly a difficult time for many writers, Orwell's sense of crisis was by no means as common as he perceived it. For example, there is virtually no mention in his writings of such contemporary novelists as Elizabeth Bowen, Joyce Cary, Graham Greene (before 1948), Evelyn Waugh (before 1949), or other serious, working novelists.

What Orwell's statements and mood reveal, I think, is his myopic preoccupation with a totalitarian threat to his culture, which fostered in him an obsessive sense of urgency and a growing pessimism about the future of the world, and these feelings of cultural apocalypse appear to have seriously undermined his confidence in the power of traditional fiction. In 1946 he wrote: "When one considers how things have gone since 1930 or thereabouts, it is not easy to believe in the survival of civilisation. . . . [However,] I think one must continue the political struggle, just as a doctor must try to save the life of a patient who is probably going to die" (4:248–49). Seeing himself as just such a beleaguered doctor, Orwell turned to the resources of an expressly political fiction. *Animal Farm* (1945) was his first imaginative work that was conceptually subordinated to a political thesis, but the facts that Orwell considered publishing it himself as a political pamphlet and that he referred to it as "a little squib" (4:95) suggest his own modest view of the work. As fine and as effective as this political fable is, it clearly does not embody the kind of imaginative power, complexity, or vitality we would expect from a novel. *Nineteen Eighty-four* (1949) is thus really a much more ambitious work, and Orwell invested much more of his obsessive anxiety into it than he had with *Animal Farm*. In fact, both the power and the flaws of his last work are derived from his continuing pessimism and his preoccupation with feelings of political-cultural apocalypse—and the disturbing power of the work cannot be denied. However, as a result of Orwell's mood the aesthetic success of the book (but not its cultural attraction to a Cold War imagination) is partly undermined by a strident, strained tone of urgency and despair, tonal notes that were not so clearly sounded in *Coming Up for Air*. The same year that he wrote *Nineteen Eighty-four* he explained his persistently melancholic state of mind by saying, "When you are on a sinking ship, your thoughts will be about sinking ships" (4:408). And it was precisely that state of mind that had so profoundly disjointed his imaginative stability and his confidence in the power of traditional fiction during the 1940s. We also need to remember that this last novel is dominated as much by the shadow of the past as it is by the shadowy world of the future, and it is in many ways a very personal, and very painful, mourning for the loss of the bourgeois, ordinary world that Orwell had celebrated in the latter half of the 1930s.

However, evidence that Orwell was not entirely satisfied with the direction of his work, and that he began to look back with growing feelings of nostalgia upon the nondidactic fiction of his early reading, is suggested in several of his essays. In his 1944 essay on Smollett he says that Smollett "accepts as a law of nature the viciousness, the nepotism and the disorder of eighteenth-century society, and therein lies his charm. Many of his best passages would be ruined by an intrusion of the moral sense" (3:246). And in his 1948 essay on Gissing, he praises Gissing's insightful depiction of the squalor of his age, but insists that it is "a point in his favour that he had no very strong moral purpose" (4:435). This nostalgia for nonideological fiction, which echoes his earlier praise for *Tropic of Cancer*, further testifies to Orwell's painful sense of his own predicament in the 1940s—when he felt overwhelmed with the burden of living in an age he saw as severed from history and from his own liberal-bourgeois tradition, and was more unable than unwilling to find relief from his obsession with a political and cultural apocalypse. Laurence Brander reports that during the closing months of his life Orwell was "ready to turn from politics and polemics to the normal preoccupation of the literary artist in our time, the study of human relationships."[9] But whether Orwell had the imaginative resources and the confidence in his own voice to complete such a task is, I think, doubtful.

One of the most painful effects his unrelieved pressures of anxiety and pessimism seem to have had upon Orwell was that he began to doubt the vitality of his creative impulse. During the last half of the forties Orwell began to speculate repeatedly on the limitations of the writer's powers, and to associate an atmosphere of orthodoxy and power politics with the drying up of the artist's imaginative faculties. In 1946 he wrote: "A novelist does not, any more than a boxer or a ballet dancer, last for ever. He has an initial impulse which is good for three or four books, perhaps even a dozen, but which must exhaust itself sooner or later. Obviously, one cannot lay down any rigid rule, but in many cases the creative impulse seems to last for about 15 years: in a prose writer those 15 years would probably be between the ages of 30 or 45, or thereabouts" (4:253). Orwell himself had been writing fiction seriously for just about fifteen years, and his recurring concern with this topic over the last four years of his life suggests that it was disturbingly subjective. In the notebook that he kept in 1949 he made this torturous entry:

It is now . . . 16 years since my first book was published, & abt 21 years since I started publishing articles in the magazines. Throughout that time there has literally been not one day in which I did not feel that I was idling, that I was behind with the current job, & that my total output was miserably small. Even at the period when I was working 10 hours a day on a book, or turning out 4 or 5 articles a week, I have never been able to get away from this neurotic feeling, that I was wasting time. I can never get any sense of achievement out of the work that is actually in progress, because it always goes slower than I intend, & in any case I feel that a book or even an article does not exist until it is finished. But as soon as a book is finished, I begin, actually from the next day, worrying because the next one is not begun, & am haunted with the fear that there never will be a next one—that my impulse is exhausted for good & all. If I look back & count up the actual amount that I have written, then I see that my output has been respectable: but this does not reassure me, because it simply gives me the feeling that I once had an industriousness & a fertility which I have now lost. [4:510–11]

It is impossible to doubt Orwell's industriousness when one looks over his impressive output of essays and articles during the 1940s, but this painful expression of despair and exhaustion, which has no parallel during the 1930s, suggests how Orwell's obsessive cultural pessimism became paralytically intertwined with his imaginative stability. And as such, this feeling of exhaustion would seem to be the logical climax of the personal and cultural crisis that he began to experience at the end of 1939.

Perhaps a final significant insight into Orwell's problematic situation during the 1940s is contained in his statement that "good novels are not written by orthodoxy-sniffers, nor by people who are conscience-stricken about their own unorthodoxy. Good novels are written by people who are not *frightened*" (1:519). Orwell was neither an "orthodoxy-sniffer" nor in a crisis about his own unorthodoxy, but he was *frightened* during the 1940s about the future of his culture and the survival of the liberal-bourgeois tradition that had nurtured his sensibility, values, and sense of self. Although these anxieties led to the writing of two of the most influential political fictions in English this century, he continued to affirm the value of a nonideological tradition of the novel and to celebrate the normative values of English cultural life. Indeed, he remained committed to a manifestly liberal tradition of the artist: he continued to see art as a means of enlarging man's sympathies and testifying to his humanity, and to see the writer as a central social intelligence, capable of affecting human awareness, transmitting moral values, influencing the order and direction of his society, and celebrating the values and vitality of the common, ordinary man. And it is for these reasons, and not simply because of his last two works, that Orwell continues to speak to us with so much vigor and clarity. Yet the course of his career testifies with painful authority to the dilemmas this liberal writer experienced as he struggled to hold in precarious balance his imaginative stability amidst a time of political trauma and what he saw as cultural disintegration. Finally, Orwell must be seen as a casualty of the "mental climate" he had so prophetically described in 1939.[10]

1. Alex Zwerdling, *Orwell and the Left* (New Haven, Conn.: Yale University Press, 1974), pp. 170–75.

2. George Orwell, *The Collected Essays, Journalism, and Letters of George Orwell*, ed. Sonia Orwell and Ian Angus, 4 vols. (New York: Harcourt, Brace & World, 1968), 1:25. All subsequent references included parenthetically in the text are to this work.

3. Orwell was especially hostile to W. H. Auden and Stephen Spender, whom he saw as representative of what he called "parlour Bolsheviks." When Orwell finally met Spender early in 1938 he found that he liked him, but this did not prevent him from continuing to negatively identify him with "Auden & Co." in his 1939 essay "Inside the Whale."

4. Victor Gallancz, *More for Timothy* (London: Gollancz, 1953), p. 356.

5. *Fact*, no. 20 (1938), p. 75.

6. Edward Upward, "Sketch for a Marxist Interpretation of Literature," *The Mind in Chains: Socialism and the Cultural Revolution*, ed. C. Day Lewis (London: Frederick Muller, 1937), p. 52.

7. Orwell's rancor for the privileged intelligentsia (he refers to them as "those moneyed beasts" in one novel) had complex, deep-seated sources, both social and temperamental. His posthumously published essay "Such, Such Were the Joys," reveals his early, painful sense of alienation from the privileged boys among whom he was educated; and Peter Stansky and William Abrahams's *The Unknown Orwell* and Bernard Crick's *George Orwell* have provided further insight into some of the psychological forces of Orwell's early years. But there is still a great deal that needs to be explained about the dynamics of Orwell's personality, imagination, and temperament, and I think Orwellian studies are at the point where greater psychological study of Orwell and his career would be invaluable, and is likely to appear.

8. There has been very little written about this planned work, and only some sixteen pages of notes for it exist in the Orwell Archive in the University of London library. For a brief discussion of the notes, and speculation on Orwell's intentions, see Bernard Crick's *George Orwell* (Boston: Little, Brown, 1980), pp. 262–63.

9. Laurence Brander, *George Orwell* (London: Longmans, 1954), p. 10.

10. Support received from the Research Grants Committee of the University of Alabama is gratefully acknowledged.

The Poem That Failed: The Auden Group's Retreat from Political Verse

Thomas Mallon

Vassar College

I N 1957 C. Day Lewis published *Pegasus*, a somewhat doleful and chastened book of poems. One of them, "The Committee," characterizes the doodling, fact-loving, axe-grinding—and yet still "public-spirited"—members of a political body. Flies buzz and seasons change as they do their work, but not much else happens:

> So the committee met again, and again
> Nailed themselves to the never-much-altered agenda,
> Making their points as to the manner born,
> Hammering them home with the skill of long practice.[1]

The "boring meeting" of Auden's famous "Spain," something that was to be today's wearisome price for tomorrow's political and moral profit, has turned, in the intervening twenty years, eternal. In Auden's poem the odds were on success; in Day Lewis's they are on failure, or, at best, continuance of the way things are.

This is not the future Day Lewis imagined at the start of his career in the early 1930s. In "The Road These Times Must Take" (a sonnet he would later exclude from his *Collected Poems*, just as Auden would exclude "Spain" from his), Day Lewis reverently described a Communist and ended a sestet of imperatives with these lines: "Mark him, workers, and all who wish the world aright— / He is what your sons will be, the road

these times must take."[2] Less than a decade later, many of those
workers lay dead under the rubble of the Blitz. They had not in
the meantime paid much attention to Day Lewis's call, and, in a
wartime poem entitled "The Dead," the poet realized he could
not blame them. In fact, he offered them an embarrassed apol-
ogy:

> Still, they have made us eat
> Our knowing words, who rose and paid
> The bill for the whole party with their uncounted courage.
> And if they chose the dearer consolations
> Of living—the bar, the dog race, the discreet
> Establishment—and let Karl Marx and Freud go hang,
> Now they are dead, who can dispute their choice?
> Not I, nor even Fate.[3]

The points at which left-wing men and women lost their faith
in a collective future varied during the frantic and appalling
events of the late 1930s. Perhaps Munich, perhaps the Nazi-
Soviet pact, perhaps only the Blitz itself first caused them to
turn from an optimistic preoccupation with a more just future
for Europe and mankind to a more somber concern with survival. Whichever the condition, five years of war acted as a
steadily pounding pestle to their opposition politics, and continuing revelations about the true state of affairs in the Soviet
Union made Communism into "the god that failed." Such personal histories of disillusionment as those collected by Richard
Crossman in his famous volume of that title became a literary
genre unto themselves. As Mary McCarthy wrote in her 1953
essay "My Confession": "Every age has a keyhole to which its
eye is pasted. Spicy court-memoirs, the lives of gallant ladies,
recollections of an ex-nun, a monk's confession, an atheist's
repentance, true-to-life accounts of prostitution and bastardy
gave our ancestors a penny peep into the forbidden room. In
our own day, this type of sensational fact-fiction is being produced largely by ex-Communists. Public curiosity shows an almost prurient avidity for the details of political defloration."[4]
Some of the English political poets of the thirties, including
those of the Auden group ("MacSpaunday"), left behind their
own prose memoirs (largely sober and honest ones) of encounters with and retreats from left-wing politics. It has become a
common critical formula to think of some of them as having
had two careers—we comfortably speak of the early and the

later Day Lewis, the early and the later Spender, and so on. It is
their retreat from political poetry that more than anything else
marks the "second phase" of their careers.

The change was wounding and thorough. In 1937 the young
Communist poet-critic Christopher Caudwell wrote in his book
Illusion and Reality: A Study of the Sources of Poetry that "it is
possible to dream with accuracy of the future."[5] Although
Caudwell was far more doctrinaire than most of those we have
come to think of as the Auden group (he found them, even in
their most political years, to be too concerned with personal
liberty and bourgeois artistic freedom), his notion of dreaming
with accuracy is a lyrically apt characterization of much of their
poetry of the 1930s, in which they envisioned a precise new
world of economic justice and unfettered imagination spring-
ing, after a death struggle, from the old. But Caudwell himself
was killed in Spain the year his book was published, and just
three years later many British readers and critics, wholly en-
gulfed in war, had ceased wrangling over the merits of a political function for poetry and were instead hoping for a new
flowering of Rupert Brookes. They were asking, "Where are
the war poets?" The joking answer to this question was, "Killed
in Spain," but more to the point was Day Lewis's brief and bitter
answer in a poem that took the question for its title:

> They who in folly or mere greed
> Enslaved religion, markets, laws,
> Borrow our language now and bid
> Us to speak up in freedom's cause.
>
> It is the logic of our times,
> No subject for immortal verse—
> That we who lived by honest dreams
> Defend the bad against the worse.[6]

In the face of possible destruction by Fascism there was little
the poet could do about carrying on his crusade for a world
better than the one immediately threatened. In that sense the
Establishment against which he had so recently been in rebellion had him over a literary and moral barrel. First things first
became the poetic order of the day; political criticism and visions had to be put on the back burner while Armageddon was
rapping at the kitchen door. Later, the reasoning went, they
could be returned to.

But the poets of the Auden group never really returned to

those simmering visions. Their radical poems of the thirties became closed books. They moved on to subjects and styles very different—indeed, to subjects and styles of which they would earlier have been skeptical or dismissive. When they recalled their youthful work they were liable to be self-mocking or self-explaining. The first attitude is found in Day Lewis's "A Letter from Rome," from his book *An Italian Visit* (1953):

> We who 'flowered' in the Thirties
> Were an odd lot; sceptical yet susceptible,
> Dour though enthusiastic, horizon-addicts
> And future-fans, terribly apt to ask what
> Our all-very-fine sensations were in aid of.
> We did not, you will remember, come to coo.[7].

In Stephen Spender's even later poem "A Political Generation," we read the second attitude; an appeal is made for critical understanding of the political poets' early work and circumstances:

> When they put pen
> To paper, in those times,
> They knew their written
> Ten lines with five rhymes,
> Before the reader had turned
> The page over, might have burned.
>
> With such doubts, how could they doubt
> Their duty—to write
> Poems that put fires out
> To keep lights alight?
> So, putting first things first,
> They did their best to write their worst.[8]

The last line of Spender's poem is a close, and probably intentional, play on the last line of "Where Are the War Poets?" Its tone, however, is no longer one of bitterness and defeat, as Day Lewis's was in 1940, but instead a mixture of pride, forgiveness, and even amusement. It is the tone of a man looking back on events that are now history, and rather distant history at that.

Most current readers of twentieth-century British poetry can quote from Auden's "Spain," or Spender's "I think continually of those who were truly great," or Day Lewis's "The Conflict," partly because their heroic optimism and "political" content make them unusual, even exotic, decades later. Often less familiar are those poems from during and after the Second World War which look back at the work of the thirties and attempt to evaluate its intentions, its overreachings, its moral successes and failures. Just as "thirties poetry" has become an historically sealed subgenre, there exists a group of wartime and postwar poems by the same writers that form, in effect, a revision of thirties aesthetics. The dramatic shift in focus that occurs during the war years in the work of Day Lewis and Spender is especially worth looking at. Auden's work, which was always more varied and complex than theirs, can be seen to change less suddenly, but in the end no less surely, and also invites rereading along these lines. In addition, why this "revisionism" hardly concerned Louis MacNeice (grouped sometimes so perplexingly with the other three) at all needs investigation if we are fairly to judge work and careers that are (with the happy exception of Spender's) receding further and further into the past.

One can gain a remarkably vivid sense of the 1930s political ethos from which these English writers would retreat by reopening the October 1934 issue of Geoffrey Grigson's *New Verse,* which published the responses of twenty poets (English and American) to "An Enquiry" made up of six questions about their mission and vocation. There is something touchingly archaic about ones like "6   As a Poet what distinguishes you, do you think, from an ordinary man?"[9] The question is a perfectly good one; it is merely seeing the number 6 before it that appeals to the affectionate side of our historical awareness. For this was an age of quantification, the springtime of sociology and market research. Malcolm Muggeridge has written of the thirties' "craving for facts" and questionnaires;[10] Bernard Bergonzi has pointed out, in *Reading the Thirties,* that Auden's precise adjectives and "classificatory vision" were bound to be attractive in an intellectual climate intrigued by Five-Year Plans, Cole Porter's cataloging lyrics, and Charles Madge's "Mass Observation"—the do-it-yourself gathering of sociological data that *New Verse* itself encouraged.[11] In fact, in chiding those who did not respond to his enquiry, Grigson criticized outmoded resistance to methodical thinking about art: "The English individual-romantic, let us affirm without ill will, dislikes the categorical prod of any question" (p. 2).

But prod Grigson did, from a number of directions. The fifth question he put to the poets was this: "Do you take your stand with any political or politico-economic party or creed?" (p. 2). The responses he received illustrated not only the conspicuous political awareness of the English respondents, but also an appreciable difference between them and their American counterparts on this score. The average American response was not nearly so politically committed as the typical English one. Conrad Aiken said simply, "No" (p. 13); Wallace Stevens said, "I am afraid that I don't" (p. 15), his phrasing more the result, one suspects, of politeness than real regret; e. e. cummings (p. 11) referred the editors to a passage in his *Eimi* that scoffs at a "measurable universe"; and Marianne Moore said, "No, but I am conservative; opposed to regimentation" (p. 16). Even William Carlos Williams, who said he was "inclined to side with the [Social Credit] proposals of Major Douglas," made "No" the first sentence of his answer (p. 16). Answers from Robinson Jeffers and Archibald MacLeish arrived too late for the October issue, but were printed in December: the first was "No," and the second was "No, I suffer the universal qualm but I am unable to take any of the nostrums. . . . The Politeraryat is a sad sight."[12] The only American to take his stand, once more, was Allen Tate, who compared the Southern Agrarian Movement to the Distributist Movement in England. But even he issued a warning about political poetry: "Doubtless the same assumptions underlie my verse and my political ideas; but it is fatal to put the one at the service of the other" (p. 20).

Hesitancy over such enlistment, and over political involvement in general, was not much shared by the English. Herbert Read and some others did say no, and Robert Graves was predictably irascible ("I now fight nobody's battles but my own," p. 6), but a sense of political obligation was the more usual response, even from those poets we think of as primarily religious- or aesthetic-minded, such as Edwin Muir, Dylan Thomas, and David Gascoyne. Muir advocated the ideas of Major Douglas. The very young Thomas, sounding more like the young Day Lewis than the author of the neo-Romantic poems the world would soon know so well, said "only through . . . an essentially revolutionary body can there be the possibility of a communal art" (p. 9). And the even younger Gascoyne (only eighteen) wrote: "My political feelings are not yet sufficiently developed or matured for me to be able to answer this question, beyond saying that I have the strongest possible sympathy with left-wing revolutionary movements" (p. 12). The important point here is that even this young Surrealist-influenced poet felt that he *should* be developing his political "feelings," and that those feelings were not a source of danger, as they seemed to be for the Americans, but rather a sign of strength.

This was the English literary-ideological climate in which the Auden group was working during the middle of the decade, and it is ironic that of the four who gave syllables to the "Mac-Spaunday" acronym only MacNeice, the least political, responded directly to the questionnaire. When it came to stating whether or not he took a political stand, he replied, in an almost American fashion, "No. In weaker moments I wish I could" (p. 7). Nothing could more clearly state his position. He was hardly a complacent man; he elsewhere expressed his own desire to "smash the aquarium" of the status quo.[13] But he resisted the impulse to "sink [his] ego" in ideology—those "weaker moments" he refers to in his response to the "Enquiry." When Grigson put together a collection of essays called *The Arts To-day,* a year after the *New Verse* questionnaire, MacNeice was chosen to write the section called "Poetry." He declared that the British were "still suffering from Shavianism, the heresy that the highest work of art is the pamphlet."[14] And he offered critical estimates of the youthful Auden, Spender, and Day Lewis that stand up remarkably well almost half a century later:

> The three most interesting poets in *New Signatures* are W. H. Auden, Stephen Spender and Cecil Day-Lewis; all three in their poems are implied communists and often propagandists. Like all propagandists (cp. Shelley) they sometimes make themselves ridiculous. Auden is often saved by his technical concentration and Spender by his technical economy but Day-Lewis, who writes longer and looser works and has not much sense of humour, has committed lamentable ineptitudes while preaching for the cause.[15]

Returning to the critical literature of the thirties, one finds MacNeice standing very much on his own ground. When he writes that politics should remain "ancillary" to poetry in any political verse, he has the ring of certainty. When Spender and Day Lewis talk about the seamless marriage of those two elements, they sound like matchmakers trying to hide their qualms.

In "The Cave of Making," a poem Auden dedicated to Mac-
Neice's memory in the 1960s, he wrote:

> More than ever
> life-out-there is goodly, miraculous, lovable,
>   but we shan't, not since Stalin and Hitler,
> trust ourselves ever again: we know that, subjectively,
>   all is possible.[16]

One reads this and is a bit troubled by the "we"; the pronoun
literally refers to the living, but there is a sense that it is meant
also to enfold Auden and MacNeice as companions of temperament and generation. And yet the understanding that we cannot trust ourselves, that we have to take pleasure in the concrete things of this world even as we recognize our capacity for
enormity, is something MacNeice understood in 1934, and
which Auden was not finally convinced of until years later. The
kind of celebration of things and friends and domestic rituals
that one finds in *About the House,* in which "The Cave of Making" appeared, one finds going on in MacNeice even in such
works of dread as *Autumn Journal* (1939). Refuge is taken in
dailiness and the senses, the "dearer consolations" Day Lewis
will forgive the wartime dead for pursuing; grander schemes
and solutions are distrusted. MacNeice writes affectingly about
Spain, and against an economic system "that gives a few at
fancy prices / Their fancy lives," but he is more consistently
fearful than others that "freedom means the power to order,
and that in order / To preserve the values dear to the élite / The
élite must remain a few." He says this fear "must be suppressed" if we are to have faith in action and in the future, but
his poetry toughly glistens with the intellectual honesty of his
inability to whistle that fear away.[17] He proposes a revivifying
sleep at the end of *Autumn Journal,* but he can't prescribe much
beyond that for his country.

MacNeice's politics may not get the world very far, and con-
sistency may be the hobgoblin Emerson thought it was, but his
early attitudes kept MacNeice from having to write a poetry of
second thoughts after the start of the war. He had no optimism
to retract, no politics to recant. For Auden, Spender, and Day
Lewis it was another matter. By the mid-1930s they had taken
to articulating possibilities for a political poetry so frequently
that their failure to respond to the *New Verse* enquiry may have
been for fear of redundancy.

Indeed, Day Lewis's only response to Grigson's questionnaire was that "several of the questions . . . are dealt with indirectly in my book."[18] The new volume he was referring to was *A Hope for Poetry* (1934), which was more or less "committed" in its poetic outlook, but managed to avoid shrillness. Day Lewis found room to praise MacNeice, and he saved his only real scorn for Dada and Surrealism. Poetry might be useful to revolution, but he does not define it as revolutionary. A year later, however, in a Hogarth Press pamphlet called *Revolution in Writing,* he reached as far and fancifully leftwards as he ever would, setting forth the following extraordinary recipe for the proletarian poet whose appearance was so frequently awaited in the thirties:

> If the writing of poetry is his natural activity (and he will soon find that out), all he needs is an English dictionary and a thorough soaking in the English poets. After that, it is a matter of compelling an alien tradition into his own service, just as the U.S.S.R. pressed the industrial technique of capitalist Europe into the service of Socialism.[19]

This urge to simplify, to declare things possible and insist on action, is the keynote of Day Lewis's thirties verse. In "The Conflict" (one of the few poems of this period he would later consider to be of lasting value) he gives up any personal and aesthetic reservations about joining the "red advance of life," because "only ghosts can live / Between two fires";[20] he ends the battle between "the poetic self and the rest of the man" that he describes in *A Hope for Poetry.*[21] Such a conflict, he argued there, is healthful because it can produce good poetry as the two sides fight and then move toward reconciliation. In *The Destructive Element* Spender praised "The Conflict," noting that while "the simplification of issues might seem to some people premature, if not grotesque," the poem was of value because it showed a struggle between two worlds that was "*real*—as real as the descriptions of environment in novels . . . the material of the poem is life."[22] But Spender is only guilty of further simplification here. The greatest poetry of ideas, from Donne through Emily Dickinson, nearly always arises out of tension, but the conflict in "The Conflict" is a false one: there is a bias in favor of one life (or self) from the start. The outcome is fast and predictable. The poetic dice are loaded from the first stanza.

We don't see a poet working out a conflict in the course of a poem; we see a poet remembering his quick dispatch of a past tension, and offering a bromide to the reader. Instead of taut reconciliation we end with the inevitable triumph of the "red advance." This false conflict (false from the standpoint of creative tension) is the subject of a number of thirties poems—in fact, along with "The Conflict," Day Lewis later chose "In Me Two Worlds" as a poem of enduring worth from this period.[23] In that poem the two selves, traditional and revolutionary, may still be at a kind of war in the final stanza, but the imagery puts the moral weight squarely on the side of the latter.

In the 1940s Day Lewis retreats from ideology and comes to write a poetry wherein tension is genuinely creative, and where an outcome is not premeditated. An absolute repentance of his political phase would have been as much a simplification as that phase itself, and he wisely, indeed nobly, refused to make such a move (even if it meant continuing to value poems like "The Conflict"). But he did try to work out a more complex and mature balance of past and present, pessimism and optimism. "Juvenilia" looks back on his early self and work, and tries to assimilate those things to their present equivalents:

> What links the real to the wraith?
> My self repudiates myself of yesterday;
> But the words it lived in and cast like a shell keep faith
> With that dead self always.
> And if aught holds true between me and you,
> It is the heart whose prism can break
> Life's primal rays
> Into a spectrum of passionate tones, and awake
> Fresh blossom for truth to swell and sway.[24]

The "red advance of life" gives way to an acceptance of its whole range of colors.

In "New Year's Eve" (like "Juvenilia" from the mid-1940s), the poet accepts time as something he must work with. History is no longer to be brought to heel by politics; rather, the vast expanses of time are to be offered the poet's awed but willing wings:

> Ring bells for here and now.
> Time's your condition; and in time alone
> May man, full grown, reach out over the void
> A rapt, creator's wing.[25]

The "Meditation" section of this poem, with its emphasis on sensory, concrete experience, its embrace of the present, brings Day Lewis to a style and perspective MacNeice had achieved nearly a decade before, but they are no less welcome and in-spiriting for that. He pledges to "court the commonplace," re-solving that

> Whatever is common to life's diversity must,
> For me, be the one eternal
> Truth, or if naught is for ever, at least the medium
> Wherein I may best discern all
> The products of time, embalmed, alive, or prefigured.[26]

This is a tough optimism, not a fake and politically mandatory one.

Reading the volumes of criticism Day Lewis wrote after the thirties, one notes their increasing emphasis on the technical and retrospective—the prescriptive note of *A Hope for Poetry* and *Revolution in Writing* fades. One senses a man burnt by his early and too enthusiastic commitment to a political poetry, a man whose gradual acceptance of ambiguity and true tension made him not only a better poet but a better reader as well.

Spender's political poems were not often as strident as Day Lewis's, but the changing pattern of his work from the thirties to the forties runs parallel to that of his contemporary and friend. In "Oh young men, oh young comrades" one finds the same "ghost" that was in Day Lewis's "Conflict," and the same desire to replace it with living beings wholeheartedly on one side:

> Oh comrades, step beautifully from the solid wall
> advance to rebuild and sleep with friend on hill
> advance to rebel and remember what you have
> no ghost ever had, immured in his hall.[27]

Another poem, "The Funeral," won Day Lewis's praise in *A Hope for Poetry*, much as "The Conflict" won Spender's in *The Destructive Element*.[28] In Spender's poem a group of workers ends a funeral for one of their own with, instead of sadness, the expression of happiness over how their comrade contributed to the building of the new workers' state:

> They walk home remembering the straining red flags,
> And with pennons of song still fluttering through their blood

> They speak of the World State
> With its towns like brain centres and its pulsing arteries.

The amazingly unironic epitaph Spender has the workers give their comrade is "How this one excelled all others in making driving belts." The workers are shown to be free of what Pound called the "old bitch gone in the teeth"—European civilization:

> No more are they haunted by the individual grief
> Nor the crocodile tears of European genius,
> The decline of a culture
> Mourned by scholars who dream of the ghosts of Greek boys.[29]

The antihomosexual jibe of these lines is especially distasteful when one remembers the more than faintly, and positive, homosexual tinge of the last lines of "Oh young men, oh young comrades."

It is hard to admire "The Funeral" any more than "The Conflict." Its pseudo-robustness and lack of subtlety bespeak a young man's quick fantasy more than a mature poet's ripe imagining. But Spender did well to preserve the poem in his *Collected Poems*, if only because it serves his later, and better, work by the contrast it provides. Spender, like Day Lewis, moved on to greater complexity and thoughtfulness in the work he did after the start of the Second World War. *Explorations*, a series of sonnets he published in 1944 (and somewhat revised in the *Collected Poems*) was dedicated to Day Lewis, and is very similar in spirit to "New Year's Eve," which Day Lewis was composing in the same period. The poet retains the admirable ambition of building "the human city," but knows it is achieved not simply by happy makers of driving belts happily buried by their comrades, but by a complex acceptance of the past along with the present and future. History is now not something to be neatly unfurled, a carpet leading to paradise, but an almost mystical blend of eras and states of mind. Using the same image of the "wing" that Day Lewis used in "New Year's Eve," Spender, too, calls for an awareness that will make itself vulnerable to time's varied manifestations:

> The Spirit of present, past, futurity
> Seeks through the many-headed wills
> To build the invisible visible city.
> Shut in himself, each blind, beaked subject kills
> His neighbour and himself, and shuts out pity
> For that flame-winged Creator who fulfils.[30]

Spender no longer presents the past as a flyblown memory of pathetic scholars, but rather as a mysterious and nourishing element of the present. The poem that results is more generous to its readers than bullyings like "The Funeral."

Auden, always more sly and skillful a poet than either Day Lewis or Spender, chose to revise and suppress a number of his early poems when their politics had come to embarrass him. This may have shown less courage than that sometimes displayed in the collected editions of Spender and Day Lewis, whose willingness to be emotionally and intellectually vulnerable is the chief, and admirable, hallmark of their poetry of the forties. Nevertheless, Auden's view of the world also became more capacious, more politically flexible, as time went on, and his poetry gained a richness of perspective it had not had in the thirties. The lean trickiness of his early versification may have sagged into a comfortable, and sometimes disappointing, middle-aged spread, but the later poems have a maturity and generosity that is not always present in the early work.

The lines he composed to be spoken by "Alonso to Ferdinand" in *The Sea and the Mirror* (1944) indicate the preference for a political and temperamental middle ground that came to mark his later years:

> The Way of Justice is a tightrope
> Where no prince is safe for one instant
> Unless he trust his embarrassment,
> As in his left ear the siren sings
> Meltingly of water and a night
> Where all flesh had peace, and on his right
> The efreet offers a brilliant void
> Where his mind could be perfectly clear
> And all his limitations destroyed:
> Many young princes soon disappear
> To join all the unjust kings.[31]

Limitations are accepted; embarrassment is trusted. Vulnerability, as in the middle and later poetry of Day Lewis and Spender, is prized.

Like Day Lewis and Spender, Auden did not altogether cease to comment on politics in his poetry after the political enthusiasms of the thirties began to chill. But the later comments could be more cryptic, and ultimately less ephemeral. "August 1968" is a poem of only four couplets, in which an Ogre walks among the "desperate and slain," and "drivel gushes from his lips": for all his brutal power he "cannot master Speech."[32] August 1968 was the month the Soviet Union invaded Czechoslovakia; it was also the month in which demonstrators at the Democratic National Convention in Chicago were bloodied in a "police riot" (the official language of the Walker Report). Auden's eight lines, one realizes, could apply to either event, and this should be seen as a strength rather than a weakness. By 1968 the poet's perspective was generous enough to suffer from both events at once, and set them into an allegorical language that allows for an even longer historical view.

The political phase of the Auden group has been both unduly scorned and romanticized. Orwell's slick characterization of their convictions as the "patriotism of the deracinated" ignores the fact that in many ways their early political beliefs were a genuine response to homegrown slump and squalor.[33] Conversely, their retreat from left-wing ideology was not the self-conscious revolt "against the absolute imperatives of Communist ideology" that Charles I. Glicksberg has detected.[34] They were neither so naive nor so deliberate as Orwell and Glicksberg would have them. Their poems of protest and their subsequent poems of wounded introspection were both responses— and often confused ones—to the circumstances of different decades. If the American poets showed little of the political interest of the British in Grigson's "Enquiry," it was, aside from their different tradition, because the press of Fascism was for them far more remote. And if British poems from the war seem at times almost unnaturally hushed, the particularly grisly nature of the air war, and the relatively greater absorption of all of ordinary life by the conflict, compared to that experienced by America, can be looked to as causes. The pressures of the war overwhelmed the economic and political pressures of the thirties and forced the group's attentions in new directions: during the war Spender had to put out literal fires (with the Auxiliary Fire Service), not the figurative ones mentioned in "A Political Generation." The quietism of England's "Movement" poets of the fifties (well chronicled in a recent book by Blake Morrison) was similarly conditioned by immediate social realities.

Another factor changing the Auden group's poetry between the thirties and forties was that they were simply growing older:

During the war they were mature enough to be fascinated by time's powers, not merely indignant at them. Criticism should be able to bear this fact of life as the poets themselves had to. John Lehmann has written, in the course of a generous assessment of the group, that "every artist has the right to be judged by his best" work.[35] But there is no real need to soft-pedal some of the shrill embarrassments of the thirties. If we can live with the older Wordsworth, we can bear the youthful MacSpaunday. We simply need a bit less of it; no group of writers has suffered more from criticism's insistence upon seeing them in their youth. Several years ago the National Portrait Gallery in London ran an exhibit "Young Writers of the Thirties": it is a label that will forever stick, and unfairly, too, for by the forties they may have been less photogenic but were better poets. Spender's *Explorations* and Day Lewis's *Poems 1943–1947* are sufficient testimony to that. Keats, Byron, and Shelley no doubt would have suffered the same fate had they not brought together actual circumstance and critical fancy by dying young.

Finally, the Auden group (which never gathered in the same room until after the Second World War) would be better served by having even their most artless political poetry seen in a longer historical context.[36] As Day Lewis wrote in his memoirs: "so far as we were imagining through our poetry a society whose values the poet could identify himself with, we were classical by intention."[37] Thirties political poetry was not *sui generis*. It resulted from historical and biographical circumstances. It has been, however, its practitioners' misfortune that the circumstantial mixture was so exotic as to make criticism pay too little attention to the finer work they would later produce. That poets will turn their eyes and voices to the political life of their times is something to be understood and wished; that strong ideology carries aesthetic perils is something that criticism cannot ignore. The poets of the Auden group provide unusually vivid illustrations of political engagement, aesthetic injury—and prudent retreat to richer ground.

1. C. Day Lewis, "The Committee," in *Pegasus and Other Poems* (London: Jonathan Cape, 1957), p. 25.

2. C. Day Lewis, "The Road These Times Must Take," *Left Review* 1 (November 1934): 35.

3. C. Day Lewis, "The Dead," in *Collected Poems of C. Day Lewis* (London: Jonathan Cape with The Hogarth Press, 1954), p. 232.

4. Mary McCarthy, "My Confession," in *On the Contrary* (New York: Farrar, Straus and Cudahy, 1961), p. 75.

5. Christopher Caudwell, *Illusion and Reality: A Study of the Sources of Poetry* (London: Macmillan, 1937), p. 305.

6. Day Lewis, "Where Are the War Poets?," *Collected Poems*, p. 228.

7. Day Lewis, "A Letter from Rome," *Collected Poems*, p. 322.

8. Stephen Spender, "A Political Generation," in *The Generous Days* (New York: Random House, 1971), p. 40.

9. "An Enquiry," *New Verse*, no. 11 (October 1934), pp. 2–20, 22. Subsequent citations of this issue are made by page number only in parentheses within the text.

10. Malcolm Muggeridge, *The Thirties: 1930–1940 in Great Britain* (London: Collins, 1967), p. 284. First published in 1940.

11. Bernard Bergonzi, *Reading the Thirties: Texts and Contexts* (Pittsburgh, Pa.: University of Pittsburgh Press, 1978), pp. 51–52.

12. *New Verse*, no. 12 (December 1934), p. 18.

13. Louis MacNeice, *The Strings Are False: An Unfinished Autobiography* (London: Faber & Faber, 1965), p. 146.

14. Louis MacNeice, "Poetry," in *The Arts To-day*, ed. Geoffrey Grigson (London: John Lane, The Bodley Head, 1935), p. 58.

15. Ibid., pp. 44–45.

16. W. H. Auden, "The Cave of Making," in *Collected Poems*, ed. Edward Mendelson (New York: Random House, 1976), pp. 521–22.

17. Louis MacNeice, *Autumn Journal* (New York: Random House, 1940), section iii, pp. 174–75.

18. *New Verse*, no. 11 (October 1934), p. 2.

19. C. Day Lewis, *Revolution in Writing* (1935); 2d ed. (London: Hogarth Press, 1938), p. 44.

20. Day Lewis, "The Conflict," *Collected Poems*, p. 128. In his memoirs, *The Buried Day* (New York: Harper & Bros., 1960), Day Lewis selects "The Conflict" and "In Me Two Worlds" as poems from his political phase that had lasting merit.

21. C. Day Lewis, *A Hope for Poetry* (1934); 7th ed. (Oxford: Basil Blackwell, 1945), p. 54.

22. Stephen Spender, *The Destructive Element: A Study of Modern Writers and Beliefs* (London: Jonathan Cape, 1935), p. 227.

23. Day Lewis, *The Buried Day*, p. 213.

24. Day Lewis, "Juvenilia," *Collected Poems*, pp. 248–49.

25. Day Lewis, "New Year's Eve," *Collected Poems*, p. 274.

26. Ibid., pp. 277–78.

27. Stephen Spender, "Oh young men, oh young comrades," *Collected Poems, 1928–1953* (London: Faber & Faber, 1955), p. 46.

28. Day Lewis, *A Hope for Poetry*, pp. 56–57.

29. Spender, "The Funeral," *Collected Poems*, p. 53.

30. Spender, "Explorations," Section V, *Collected Poems*, p. 151.

31. Auden, "The Sea and the Mirror," *Collected Poems*, p. 321. This section of "The Sea and the Mirror" is entitled "Alonso to Ferdinand" in *Selected Poetry of W. H. Auden*, Modern Library, 1959, and I am grateful to Edward Mendelson for originally drawing my attention to it.

32. Auden, "August 1968," *Collected Poems*, p. 604.

33. George Orwell, "Inside the Whale," in *A Collection of Essays* (Garden City, N.Y.: Doubleday, 1954), p. 242.

34. Charles I. Glicksberg, *The Literature of Commitment* (Lewisburg, Pa.: Bucknell University Press, 1976), p. 254.

35. John Lehmann, *In My Own Time: Memoirs of a Literary Life* (Boston: Little, Brown, 1969), p. 166.

36. See John Press, *A Map of Modern English Verse* (London: Oxford University Press, 1969), pp. 199–200. Press mentions a meeting of Auden, Day Lewis, and Spender in 1947.

37. Day Lewis, *The Buried Day*, p. 217.

Critics and Ideology

Billy Budd and the Judgment of Silence

Brook Thomas
University of Hawaii

If our judgements approve the war that is but coincidence
—Melville, *Billy Budd*

A critic would have to be very innocent today to believe in the possibility of an innocent encounter with a text. All readings, it seems certain, have been mediated by interpretive schemas that are conditioned by and help condition the ideologies of a society. There are no innocent readings. One who attempts one is revealing his own ideological assumptions. If his reading does not self-consciously announce its awareness of those assumptions, there will be a critic available to point them out. That critic's reading of a critic reading is in turn subject to another reading that will expose another set of assumptions, and so on.

The complications multiply. There is not even a shared agreement as to what we mean by ideology. Do we mean a system of beliefs or a false consciousness, or do we reject both definitions? Can we speak of a science/ideology opposition or is science itself an ideology? Is ideology a mode of discourse or a lived experience? Our choice of a definition of ideology betrays an ideology.

There is even an unexamined (but of course it has been examined) ideology to the proliferation of critics reading critics. Economic necessity dictates that critics produce articles in order to survive. A belief in the impossibility of an innocent encounter with a text creates a situation that can justify the endless production of articles and books by the "nature" of the

51

discipline. Institutions, presses, and journals are established to serve that need. But once they are established, the institutions, presses, and journals that are said to answer the needs of the profession start to create the need they are said to be serving. The production and consumption of scholarship follows the logic of consumer society itself.

With all of this it seems to be a testament to the power of what used to be called primary texts that some of us still find ourselves interested in them, even if that interest is not without self-interest. In fact, the awareness that any act of reading is in some ways self-interested allows a relatively new approach to the use of literary texts to study ideology. The traditional ideological study adheres to the reflection theory of literature and maintains that the faithful representation of a world in literature reflects the historical conditions and resultant ideology of the age that produced it.[1] Produced by the material conditions of a society, a literary text becomes a special kind of commodity in that it speaks not only to but also about the conditions of its own production.[2] To this we can add the insight that a text is produced not once but many times. Every time a text is read it is reproduced; it speaks to and about the conditions leading to its reproduction through the act of reading, as well as its production through the act of writing. Thus, the encounter between a text and a reader becomes a way of studying both the ideology of the reader reading it and the world it represents. To move beyond the individual, the ways a generation of readers or a society reads its texts expose that generation's or society's ideologies, and the texts a society reads help to shape those ideologies. If we cannot have a direct encounter with a text, we can study how a text has been encountered. That study tells us something about the text, the reader of the text, and our own way of reading that encounter.[3]

My emphasis on the encounter between readers and a text indicates that I do not consider ideology simply to refer to a set of beliefs. Instead, for my working definition of ideology I will use the rather convoluted one of Anthony Giddens: "Ideology refers to the *ideological*, this being understood in terms of the capability of dominant groups or classes to make their own sectional interests appear to others as universal ones."[4] The advantage of this definition is that it allows us to account for the fact that the most subtle form of ideological control is not to force people to accept a set of beliefs but to predetermine ways of seeing the world. Ideology is not something to be discovered merely by studying the literary object, since our study of an object is always mediated. Instead ideology is exposed in an encounter between ways of seeing and a world or ways of reading and a text.

This essay is about such an encounter between a text and its readers, or, more specifically, a particular reader who has studied other readings. The text is *Billy Budd,* a text concerned with innocence, judgment, and possible ways of reading. The reader is Barbara Johnson, who demystifies the possibility of innocent readings by exploring what is involved in an act of judgment. An attempt to ascertain the ideology of Johnson's "Melville's Fist: The Execution of *Billy Budd*"[5] is particularly important because her essay is an excellent example of what has come to be called a "deconstructive" reading, a strategy of reading gaining more and more influence. The text of *Billy Budd* is a good ground to test the self-interestedness of the deconstructive strategy.

In one sense Johnson's reading can be seen as an attempt to place some sort of order on the chaos raging in *Billy Budd* criticism. Controversy about the book has tended to focus not on its title character but on Captain Vere. How we read Captain Vere places us on one side of a long-standing critical debate. Should we take Vere as Melville's spokesman and accept Billy's death because innocence cannot survive in the world, or should we view Vere ironically and protest Billy's death as a condemnation of a social order that demands the death of innocence? Is the book Melville's final testament of acceptance or his final testament of resistance? Is it the acceptance of tragedy or the tragedy of acceptance?

Johnson accounts for the controversy over Vere by showing that the terms of the dispute, that is, reading Vere literally (as Melville's spokesman) or ironically, is "one of the things the story is about" (p. 574). The antagonist and protagonist in the story illustrate these two ways of reading. Billy's way of reading is literal. He reads what is on the surface. "To deal in double meanings and insinuations of any sort was quite foreign to his nature" (p. 12). Claggart, on the other hand, distrusts appearances. He reads ironically, always looking for a disparity between a surface meaning and a deeper meaning. Since the crit-

ical controversy over how to read the book is something the
book is about, "it is not enough to try to decide which of the
readings is correct. What the reader of *Billy Budd* must do is
analyze what is at stake in the very opposition between literality
and irony" (p. 574).

Not surprisingly, Captain Vere, the judge in the drama, offers a third way of reading.

> The naive or literal reader takes language at face value and treats
> signs as *motivated;* the ironic reader assumes that the relation be-
> tween sign and meaning can be *arbitrary* and that appearances are
> made to be reversed. For Vere, the functions and meanings of signs
> are neither transparent nor reversible but fixed by socially deter-
> mined *convention.* Vere's very character is determined not by a rela-
> tion between his outward appearance and his inner being but by the
> "buttons" that signify his position in society. While both Billy and
> Claggart are said to owe their character to "Nature," Vere sees his
> actions and being as meaningful only within the context of a con-
> tractual allegiance. . . . Judgment is thus for Vere a function neither
> of individual conscience nor of absolute justice but of "the rigor of
> martial law" operating *through* him. [Pp. 589–90]

Although Johnson does not call attention to the fact, Vere's
way of reading is also represented in *Billy Budd* criticism. It
appears in Charles Reich's "The Tragedy of Justice in *Billy
Budd.*"[6] Anyone familiar with Reich knows that he would not
argue that Billy must die, yet he does not condemn Captain
Vere for making that judgment. He, like Captain Vere, claims
that the law, not the captain, decides Billy's fate. "At the outset,
it is vital to note that Melville allows Vere no choice within the
terms of the law itself; if the law is obeyed, Billy must hang. . . .
We may perhaps criticize the law, but not the officer whose
'vowed responsibility' is to 'adhere to it and administer it'"
(p. 369).

What Johnson does by accounting for these three ways of
reading is to offer a fourth way of reading: a way of reading
that accounts for the different ways of reading *Billy Budd.* Her
reading would seem to be a privileged and more enlightened
reading, because it avoids the blindness of the other readings.
While the first three ways of reading take a definite stand by
judging, Johnson's way of reading tries to describe rather than
judge. With Captain Vere, "Melville seems to be presenting us
less with an *object* for judgment than with an *example* of judg-

ment" (Johnson, p. 592). What this example of judgment shows is that judgment is always "a partial reading (in both senses of the word)" (p. 597).

The partiality of judgment comes from its basic function. "The function of judgment is to convert an ambiguous situation into a decidable one. But it does so by converting a difference *within* . . . into a difference *between*. . . . A difference *between* opposing forces presupposes that the entities in conflict be knowable. A difference *within* one of the entities in question is precisely what problematizes the very *idea* of an entity in the first place, rendering the 'legal point of view' inapplicable. In studying the plays of ambiguity and binarity, Melville's story situates *its* critical difference neither within or between, but precisely in the very question of the *relation between the two* as the fundamental question of all human politics" (p. 596).

The critics who judge Captain Vere succumb to the same partiality. The critical controversy over Vere ignores the inherent ambiguity of Melville's text and tries to transform differences contained *within* the text to differences occurring *outside* the text between critics. The only way to avoid distorting the ambiguity contained within the text seems to be to adopt a strategy typical of deconstruction: the deferred judgment and interpretation.

A deferred interpretation stays "truer" to the text because any interpretation involves a judgment that halts the play of the text's inherently ambiguous language. Opponents of deconstruction might object that, if deconstruction admits that an interpretation can halt the play of language, it must also admit that language does not play by itself and, therefore, is not *inherently* ambiguous. But this notion is undercut when we try to find a fixed ground for judgment, since the ambiguity of the text's language denies us a grounds by which to judge it. Thus, the advantage of the deferred judgment is that it refuses to construct a false ground from which to judge the text and thereby allows the free play of language that denies a ground of judgment in the first place.

A close look at Johnson's reading of *Billy Budd* shows why traditional students of literature consider this strategy so threatening: it deprives them of their sacred grounds of judgment—the text. While Johnson's reading remains traditional in that it claims to stay consistent with evidence to be found within the text, it is subversive in that it undercuts the notion that staying true to the text will produce a privileged or authorized reading. Unlike a New Critical reading, Johnson's reading shows that the different readings allowed by a text cannot be woven together into an organic unity. "Truth uncompromisingly told will always have its ragged edges; hence the conclusion of such a narration is apt to be less finished than an architectural finial."[7] Since the text of *Billy Budd* can be shown to support consistent readings that are irreconcilable, Johnson shows that it is precisely *because* judgments are based on textual evidence that they lack a solid ground of authority. *Billy Budd* makes her point almost too easy because the text we have is not authorized but patched together from an unfinished manuscript. To make matters worse, the manuscript that exists seems to *support* the subversion of its own authority. As Melville makes "clear," *Billy Budd* is a work of fiction, and "the *might-have-been* is but boggy ground to build on" (*BB,* p. 27). Furthermore, as Johnson very persuasively argues, the text seems to imply that any appeal to a grounds of judgment beyond the text could be traced to another text. At the same time that it denies textual authority, Johnson's reading shows that we are locked into a textual world. To stay true to the text seems to deny that textual evidence can be a ground for judgment, and yet the only evidence we can appeal to is textual.

It goes without saying that Johnson's own reading is included in her critique. Despite its enlightened awareness about the inevitability of blindness, it refuses to grant itself a privileged status. This is shown in Johnson's discussion of the fourth reader in the text, the reader coming closest to her way of reading—the old Dansker. "A man of 'few words, many wrinkles,' and 'the complexion of an antique parchment' [*BB,* p. 50], the Dansker is the very picture of one who understands and emits ambiguous utterances" (p. 597). The Dansker "never interferes in aught and never gives advice" (*BB,* p. 77). But, as Johnson points out, the Dansker's desire to give an accurate reading of events without participating in them has political consequences; it gets Billy into trouble by having him cry out. "There now, who says that Jemmy Legs is down on me!" (*BB,* p. 56). Johnson remarks: "The transfer of knowledge is not any more innocent than the transfer of power. For it is precisely through the impossibility of finding a spot from which knowledge could be all-encompassing that the plays of political power proceed" (p. 598). All readings, even those trying to avoid the political arena, are political.

But to call all ways of reading political still leaves an important question unanswered. Because they risk a judgment, the first three readings clearly reveal their political allegiance. To read Vere literally is to accept the existing system of authority. To read Vere ironically is to undercut it. To claim that the law not Vere is responsible for Billy's death is to accept the authority of the socially accepted code of laws but to admit that laws can be changed. What, however, is the political allegiance of Johnson's way of reading, a way of reading that rather than judging tries to preserve the ambiguity of the text by ending with these sentences: "The 'deadly space' or 'difference' that runs through *Billy Budd* is not located *between* knowledge and action, performance and cognition: it is that which, within cognition, functions as an act: it is that which, within action, prevents us from ever knowing whether what we hit coincides with what we understand. And this is what makes the meaning of Melville's last work so . . . *striking*" (p. 599)?

What I find most striking about Johnson's reading, however, is how her awareness of the problematics of political understanding and action keeps her from risking error by making a judgment. If, as Johnson argues, the text of *Billy Budd* judges those who judge, it should also be added that not to judge is an act of judgment in itself. To examine the ideology of a reading of *Billy Budd* that does not judge, I want to turn from Johnson's reading to *Billy Budd* itself, since, as I suggested earlier, a unique aspect of a literary text seems to be that it judges its readers as much as its readers judge it.

But the sophistication of Johnson's reading draws attention to the difficulties involved in using an encounter with a text to study the ideology of a way of reading. Even though I might argue that the text of *Billy Budd* judges its readers while they judge it, I, no more than earlier readers, can have an immediate encounter with the text. In order to appeal to *Billy Budd* to judge Johnson's way of reading, I have to adopt my own way of reading the text. Thus, to a certain extent, it will always be my way of reading, not the text, that judges her reading. Furthermore, because Johnson has already undercut the authority of any way of reading that relies on the text as a ground for judgment, *merely* to produce another "consistent" reading in opposition to hers is not enough.[8] Instead I need to find a way of reading that can establish a basis for judgment beyond textuality. At the same time, if I hope to stay "true" to the text, I will have to demonstrate that the text itself implies that basis for judgment.

Given these complications, one of the few ways of reading available to us today that can be exposed to a deconstructive reading and not be absorbed by it is one relying on Marxist assumptions. Confronted with deconstruction, a Marxist reading has the advantage that it can agree with deconstruction's two most subversive moves: the denial of textual authority and the deconstruction of the "self."[9] Unlike deconstruction, however, a Marxist reading uses these subversive moves to judge rather than to suspend judgment. My procedure will be first to use the undercutting of textual authority in order to judge Captain Vere and then to use the deconstruction of the autonomy of the self in order to judge Captain Vere's object of judgment, Billy Budd. These two judgments will in turn provide me with a way of judging Johnson's refusal to judge. Before turning to my reading, I want to acknowledge that my judgment of not judging is by no means a judgment that escapes ideology, since, as Giddens remarks, "any type of political discourse, including Marxism, which anticipates an end to ideology, carries thereby the potentiality of becoming itself ideological."[10] In other words, because it would be ideological to claim that my particular Marxist reading at this moment in time is not also a partial reading, I will have to produce a judgment that admits the possibility of its own error while still offering its ground for judgment as the ground by which that error can be judged.

A Marxist reading can go along with and even encourage deconstruction's undercutting of textual authority because, in the political realm, the appeal to textual authority, that is, laws, has been one of the most subtle ways for dominant powers to maintain control. While the defenders of "legal, rational" systems of government place authority in an "impersonal" set of laws,[11] a Marxist can point out that the real power lies in which class writes and administers the laws. Thus, when Johnson shows that the laws Vere appeals to are not grounded in "Nature" but in rhetoric, a Marxist would agree and add the question: What is the nature of the power structure that allows Vere and Vere's way of reading a privileged position to control how those laws are written and interpreted? To answer that question we need to take a closer look at Vere's way of reading.

Johnson claims that in interpreting the law Vere is a historical reader. It would be more accurate, I think, to point out his tendencies toward legal positivism. Niklas Luhmann describes the legal positivist's view: "The law of a society is positivized when the legitimacy of pure legality is recognized, that is, when law is respected because it is made by responsible decision in accordance with definite rules. Thus, in a central question of human co-existence, arbitrariness becomes an institution."[12] The problem with this view is that it can shrink to a belief in mere legality, the parallel in literary studies being a belief in mere textuality.

Jürgen Habermas's summary of the positivist's position shows how similar it is to Vere's. For the positivist,

> the formal rules of procedures suffice as legitimizing premises of decision and require for their part no further legitimation, for they fulfill their function—to absorb uncertainty—in any case. They connect the uncertainty as to *which* decision will come about with the certainty that *some* decision will come about. The abstract imperative validity [*Sollgeltung*] of norms that can do without a material justification beyond the following of correct procedure in their origin and application serves "to stabilize behavioral expectations against disappointment and thereby to guarantee structures."[13]

What is important for Vere is that uncertainty be absorbed and that structure be guaranteed. This is best done by adherence to "formal rules and procedures" or, to use Melville's phrase, "forms and usages," which institutionalize arbitrariness. Questions of "ought" need not be considered in the human realm: when a member of the drumhead court objects that Billy "purposed neither mutiny nor homicide," Vere responds: "Beyond a court less arbitrary and more merciful than a martial one, that plea would largely extenuate. At the Last Assizes it shall acquit" (*BB*, p. 107).

But despite Vere's similarities to a legal positivist, he ultimately betrays an important difference. The legal positivist believes that it is meaningless to search behind the belief in legality for more solid ground of authority. Any claims for an authority beyond the law are "functionally necessary deceptions." Vere, to the contrary, believes that laws can be justified by appealing to the "nature" of human nature. According to Vere the human condition does not change over time.

Relying on T. E. Hulme's definition of the classicist impulse, Milton Stern summarizes Vere's conservative view of human nature as "a belief in the limited nature of human potential and the fallen nature of man and, therefore, in control and decorum and in the illusory quality of change and perfectibility" (*BB*, p. xx). Vere appeals to laws because for him they represent rationality and order and thus control irrationality and chaos. Not at all surprising in a book about reading, Vere finds justification for his beliefs in his reading. The manner in which he does so is a perfect example of a functionally necessary deception.

Vere's normal "bias" is "towards those books to which every serious mind of *superior order* occupying any active post of authority in the world, *naturally* inclines: books treating of actual men and events no matter of what era—history, biography and unconventional writers like Montaigne, who, free from cant and convention, honestly and in the spirit of commonsense philosophize upon realities" (*BB*, p. 36, my italics). Captain Vere wants books that represent the world as it is, not books that fictionalize the world. For Vere the way the world is does not change from era to era; there are timeless truths.

But the next paragraph undermines the sense of reality represented in these books. Vere loves them because they give him "confirmation of his own more reserved thoughts—confirmation which he had vainly sought in social converse" (*BB*, p. 36). Rather than choosing books that reflect a reality outside of himself, a reality confirmed by converse with others, Vere chooses books that reflect his own sense of reality. What Vere considers unconventional is just another convention. Books that seem to have an objective authority turn out to have a subjective authority. Yet it is on the basis of the reality Vere finds confirmed in these books that Vere sentences Billy Budd to death. Similarly, it is the "objective" report of Budd's death in the *News from the Mediterranean* that distorts the facts of the case. Histories and biographies are constructed from such "factual" documents as newspaper reports. Appropriately, Vere's strongest statement defending law and order is supported not by histories and biographies but by a myth. " 'With mankind, . . . forms, measured forms are everything; and that is the import couched in the story of Orpheus with his lyre spellbinding the wild denizens of the wood.' And this he once applied to the disruption of forms going on across the Channel and the consequences thereof" (*BB,* p. 130).

Vere's appeal to the necessity of order through law is a typical strategy of the conservatives of his time. As Douglas Hay writes, "The justice of English law was . . . a powerful ideological weapon in the arsenal of conservatives during the French Revolution." Convincing the lower classes plus itself of the justice of the law allowed the British propertied class that "passed one of the bloodiest penal codes in Europe to congratulate itself on its humanity."[14] People were killed but killed justly. Even the rhetoric Vere uses to condemn Billy to death follows the standard rhetoric eighteenth-century judges used to deliver their death sentences. He adopts both the stance of an impartial agent through whom the law speaks and the role of a paternalistic father holding a position of "natural" authority.

Vere's appeal to the law is successful. It achieves an important aim of the political system he represents: to eliminate ambiguity in judgments by silencing the opposition. It accomplishes its aim subtly because it uses the force of rhetoric not physical force.[15] Vere's strategy of calling the drumhead court is a perfect example of how the rhetoric of the law can be used to enlist the support of those controlled by the law's rhetoric. To call the drumhead court would seem to be precisely the opposite of silencing different points of view. Vere allows the members of the court, including a representative of the crew, to speak while he adopts the role of the impartial witness. But the men speak without a chance of reversing the judgment Vere made at the moment of the murder—" 'Struck dead by an angel of God! Yet the angel must hang!' " (*BB,* p. 95). The moment Vere drops the role of an impartial witness and adopts the role of the prosecutor his "prejudgment" (*BB,* p. 104) of Billy becomes clear. One by one he opposes the scruples of the members of the court and assigns them to a realm of silence. Captain Vere, a member of the class that wrote the laws of the land, takes on the role of witness, prosecutor, and judge. Small wonder that Billy, "a *'King's bargain'* " (*BB,* p. 88), is killed as soon as his existence is no longer seen as an asset.

Once the legal system that Vere defends as impartial is shown to be weighted in favor of the interests of his own class, the foundation for Vere's judgment of Billy collapses. No one is

better at exposing Vere's shaky foundation of judgment than
Edgar Dryden, who calls attention to those hints in the text
which suggest that rather than keeping out the irrational, subversive forces of chaos, Captain Vere's measured forms are the
most subtle disguise that the forces of chaos can adopt.

> The appalling truth of *Billy Budd* is not that innocence must be
> sacrificed to maintain the order of the world, but rather that inno-
> cence is destroyed by the forces of chaos and darkness masquerad-
> ing as "measured forms." The "Bellipotent" is the "Athee" hiding
> behind the cloak of the impostor chaplain she carries; and the
> Articles of War merely cover with an official mask the same irra-
> tional forces which are found undisguised "across the Channel."
> . . . The forces of darkness and chaos achieve their greatest success
> when they take on and use the forms which men create in order to
> convince themselves that they live in an ordered world.[16]

Dryden also points out that despite Vere's show of
"philosophic austerity," the captain "may yet have indulged in
the most secret of all passions, ambition" (*BB,* p. 132). The real
motive for Vere's condemnation of Billy Budd may not have
been to preserve order, but to gain promotion, "to avoid the
possibility of any shadow's being cast on his official reputation"
(p. 212). While Dryden admits that we will never know Vere's
secret motives, "the mere presence of ambiguity is enough to
undermine his world of 'measured forms'" (p. 212). The motives of "reasonable" actions are as difficult to know as the motives of "irrational" ones.

Once Dryden alerts us to the possibility that Captain Vere's
orderly world may be controlled by the same force as the form-
less world the captain so fears, we can reinterpret a number of
passages. Most damaging to Captain Vere's position may be the
narrator's discussion of insanity. The ship's surgeon, soon after
pronouncing Billy dead, questions Captain Vere's mental state.
Although fear of being considered insolent or being accused of
mutiny keeps him from uttering his doubts, the surgeon considers Vere's "excited exclamations so at variance with his normal manner" (*BB,* p. 96) as a sign of possible mental imbalance.
In other words, the surgeon suspects that the captain may be
"unhinged" because he deviates from his normal formal behavior.

But earlier we are given an even more frightening possibility
to consider. Trying to help us understand Claggart's character,
the narrator defines his peculiar madness.

But the thing which in eminent instances signalizes so exceptional a nature is this: though the man's even temper and discreet bearing would seem to intimate a mind peculiarly subject to the law of reason, not the less in his heart he would seem to riot in complete exemption from that law, having apparently little to do with reason further than to employ it as an ambidexter implement for effecting the irrational. That is to say: Toward the accomplishment of an aim which in wantonness of atrocity would seem to partake of the insane, he will direct a cool judgement sagacious and sound.

These men are true madmen, and of the most dangerous sort, for their lunacy is not continuous but occasional, evoked by some special object; it is protectively secretive, which is as much as to say it is self-contained, so that when moreover, most active, it is to the average mind not distinguishable from sanity, and for the reason above suggested, that whatever its aims may be—and the aim is never declared—the method and the outward proceeding are always perfectly rational. [*BB*, pp. 60–61]

If we use the technique of indirection advocated throughout the book and apply this definition of madness to Vere instead of Claggart, we have an almost perfect fit.[17] Vere's "cool judgement sagacious and sound" to condemn Billy may be the act of a true madman "of the most dangerous sort." The most dangerous madness is not the clinical sort defined by the surgeon as a variance from normal manner but the exceptional sort that retains the appearance of reason and form. Rather than a deviation from normal usage, madness can be adherence to usage. Vere's ordered world can as easily serve the irrational as control it.

Vere's personal madness can be extended to the entire society that he serves. Arguing for Budd's death, Vere eloquently reminds the officers that they owe their allegiance to the king, not to nature. But if we remember our history, we remember who was king at that time, and we remember that King George was mad. Thus we have exactly the type of upside-down world that Dryden suggests. Vere owes his allegiance to a mad king and the irrational forces of war, yet the experts considered capable of detecting insanity—the clergy and men of medicine—are under Vere's command. British rule of law and order serves the very forces of chaos and irrationality that it claims to wage war against, a war fought by either impinging on the rights of nonmilitary sailors or emptying prisons of lawbreachers. War itself becomes the master, and it is war's progeny, the Mutiny Act, defended as a product of man's reason through law, which condemns Billy Budd to death. What

makes the deceit even more complete is that Captain Vere
(along with those readers who support his stand) is probably
not aware of the madness of his position. Furthermore, no one,
not the chaplain, not Billy's fellow sailors, not even Billy himself, questions this rule by self-interestedness masquerading as
impartiality.

If we juxtapose the reading of Vere that I have offered with
Johnson's, what is most revealing is that Johnson could accept
the possibility of my reading and still refuse to judge Captain
Vere. Having recognized the partiality of any judgment, she
cannot bring herself to judge. Thus, she adopts the same stance
as the members of the crew and Billy—silence. But if my reading has any credibility, we should consider the possibility that
within the context of *Billy Budd* the stance of silence, far from
being neutral, serves the interests of the system of order that
Vere represents. Silence in the face of his judgment is what
Vere desires, and silence is what Johnson's reading delivers.
Not surprisingly, silence is also something the text of *Billy Budd*
speaks to, since its very existence comments on Melville's silence
in prose fiction thirty years prior to the writing of *Billy Budd*.
Billy Budd is a text that speaks not only to and about the conditions of its own production; it is also a text that speaks to and
about the conditions that would deny its production; that is, the
conditions that would lead a writer to adopt a stance of silence
in the face of a political system that he recognizes to be potentially repressive.
Of course, it is impossible for us to interpret Melville's thirty
years of silence with certainty. Silence itself is ambiguous. Like
the "inarticulate" murmur at the time of Billy's execution, it is
"dubious in significance" (*BB*, p. 128). But the very dubiousness
of silence should give the lie to the naive assumption that somehow silence is more innocent than speech. This assumption is
widespread in the criticism of *Billy Budd*, and it has led to an
uncritical attitude about Billy. So, having judged Captain Vere,
I now need to judge his object of judgment, Billy, whose most
striking feature is his flaw—an inability to speak in a crisis.
Billy's inability to speak out might say something about both the
reasons for Melville's thirty years of silence and Johnson's
stance of silence in refusing to judge the system that judges
Billy.

A fitting comment on the ideology of most readers of *Billy Budd* is that all the critics who condemn Captain Vere and even most who support him fail to question Billy's innocence. The only critics to question Billy's innocence are a few psychoanalytic critics, a few supporters of Vere, like James E. Miller, Jr., who writes of "The Catastrophe of Innocence,"[18] and of course our deconstructive critic—Johnson. But this widespread acceptance of Billy's innocence forgets an important fact of the story: it is exactly Billy's "innocence" that is on trial.

The acceptance of Billy's innocence is connected with a belief in an ahistorical autonomous self existing prior to society and society's system of signs. Such a belief sees Billy's innocence as a presocial force of good balancing Claggart's presocial force of evil. Billy's difficulty in speaking along with his inability to read and write seem to support this notion. The sacrifice of illiterate Billy becomes a metaphor for how language inevitably distorts the "truth." Words—a product of society—inevitably sacrifice the purity of the naturally innocent signified to the distortions of the signifier.[19] Billy seems to have his origins in a world prior to signification, a world in which gesture has priority over language.[20] The text itself seems to support the truth of gesture over language. The expression on Captain Vere's face after leaving the compartment in which he condemned Billy reveals more agony than the words he pronounces. When the chaplain prays with Billy, "the genuine Gospel was less on his tongue than in his aspect and manner towards him" (*BB*, p. 124). But any attempt to grant superiority to gesture over language is undercut by Billy striking Claggart.

In questioning Billy's innocence Johnson points to Billy's act of murder by not speaking and contrasts it with Vere's act of murder by speaking in order to argue that speaking and not speaking can have the same results. But we get a very different picture once we realize that the political structure granting Vere his privilege to murder by speaking also leads Billy to murder by not speaking. Caught in a political system that denies his speech the potential for action that the speech of those above him has, Billy can speak only through violence. Explaining why he decked Claggert, Billy maintains, " 'No, there was no malice between us. I never bore malice against the Master-at-arms. I am sorry that he is dead. I did not mean to kill him. Could I have used my tongue I would not have struck him. But he foully lied to my face and in presence of my Captain, and I had to say something, and I could only say it with a blow, God help me!'" (*BB*, p. 102). By falling back on violence to speak to Claggart's charges, Billy shows that he, as much as the master-at-arms, can be controlled by the irrational force that leads to war. Although Captain Graveling of the *Rights-of-Man* calls Billy his peacemaker, the *Bellipont's* lieutenant may be more accurate when he remarks, "'well, blessed are the peacemakers, especially the fighting peacemakers!'" (*BB*, p. 8). Billy's innocence, flawed as it is, is no guarantee against the rule of chaos and war; it may even contribute to it. Perhaps war's most effective disguise, a disguise more subtle than the disguise of rationality, is a masquerade as innocence.

To question Billy's innocence is to show how the desire for innocence helps the ruling class maintain power. The day following his impressment, Billy witnesses his first "formal gang-way-punishment." Rather than protesting the violence of the beating, Billy is so impressed by the scene that he resolves "never through remissness would he make himself liable to such a visitation or do or omit aught that might merit even verbal reproof" (*BB*, p. 49). Billy's desire to avoid the judgment meted out to sailors who disobey the accepted forms and usages of the navy makes him easy to control because it renders him silent. Silence in *Billy Budd,* as it does in *Moby Dick,* signals consent to the existing system of authority. In *Moby Dick* it is when Starbuck can no longer speak that Ahab knows he has controlled him: "Speak, but speak!—Aye, aye! thy silence, then, *that* voices thee. . . . Starbuck now is mine; cannot oppose me now, without rebellion."[21] Unable to speak against Ahab, Starbuck can only contemplate violent revenge. Unable to commit violence, Starbuck continues to acquiesce. Billy of course does commit a violent act, but, unconscious, it is easily contained by Captain Vere's system of rhetorical authority, since it is caused by Billy's fear that Captain Vere will not consider him innocent. Just as Starbuck's weakness is a conscience that would judge him for committing violence against his captain, so Billy's weakness is his juvenile "good nature" that wants to please.

"Now Billy, like sundry other essentially good-natured ones, had some of the weaknesses inseparable from essential good nature; and among these was a reluctance, almost an incapacity of plumply saying *no* to an abrupt proposition not obviously absurd, on the face of it, nor obviously unfriendly, nor iniquitous" (*BB*, p. 69). The inability to say no is Billy's biggest flaw, a flaw that becomes more significant when we compare Billy to Jack Chase, to whom the book is dedicated. Chase, unlike Billy, was a man who said no to an exploitive order and achieved reform. Chase, like the Hawthorne Melville so admired, knew how to say "No, in thunder."[22] Billy, on the other hand, given the "order" that condemns him to death, "in silence mechanically obeyed" (*BB*, p. 94).

Billy's failure to speak out denies him the role promised to him early in the book, the role of the Handsome Sailor. Although Billy has "as much of masculine beauty as one can expect anywhere to see," he fails to fit the role allotted to him because of his vocal defect. How important this defect becomes is indicated by the narrator's early description of the Handsome Sailor's tales of prowess. "Ashore he was the champion; afloat the spokesman; on every suitable occasion always foremost" (*BB*, pp. 4–5). While Billy is indeed a foretopman, he is by no means a spokesman.[23] In writing Billy's story, however, Melville becomes a spokesman once again.

It may not be accidental that in order to write a story breaking thirty years of silence in prose fiction Melville had to kill off the figure in his story representing an innocence prior to speech. If we accept a commonplace interpretation of Melville's silence in prose fiction, his silence is linked to a desire for innocence similar to Billy's.[24] This interpretation argues that, beginning his career as a writer with the naive belief that he could use the forms of fiction to tell the Truth, Melville soon came to realize that his task was not an easy one. Before he could tell the Truth, he had to contend with false versions of it already accepted by the world. While Truth always has its ragged edges, the versions of Truth accepted by the world tied those edges together into formal unities. Using the forms of fiction Melville could expose the masquerade of false versions of Truth, but he could not construct a version that did not succumb to his own critique. He himself relied on the formal qualities of art that he had shown to lead to distortions. Confronted with this dilemma, Melville might indeed choose silence as his only alternative. It seems more innocent not to write at all than to perpetuate distortions of the Truth.

If this interpretaton is accurate, a major factor causing Melville's silence is his own desire innocently to state the Truth. Once the notion of a presocial Truth is rejected, however, silence loses its claim to innocence. If there is no Truth, the only way to truths may be through discourse. Discourse, in turn, takes place within a social context. If that social context includes ideological restraints forcing or inviting silence, the interests of truth are not served.[25]

At this point, it is important to note the similarity between the stance of silence that I claim Melville rejects and the stance of silence Johnson adopts in her refusal to judge. Just as the earlier Melville could expose how existing versions of the Truth distort the Truth, so can Johnson expose how existing readings of *Billy Budd* distort the text. Neither, however, can escape his or her own critique. Thus, presented with a text whose "truth" will always be distorted by a reading imposing formal closure, Johnson denies herself the authority to judge and adopts the strategy of a deferred interpretation—a stance, like the Dansker's, of silence. Since to judge is to lay oneself open to judgment (including one's own), not to judge seems to be a way to escape judgment. But, as I have tried to show through the example of Billy Budd, in writing again, Melville judges precisely that desire to escape judgment. Curiously enough, Johnson, with her sophisticated way of reading, shares a similarity with naive Billy. Both have a desire to maintain an innocence that Melville's text shows not to exist. In both cases the desire involves an attempt to escape history.

Since it is on the role of history in interpretation that I disagree most strongly with Johnson, it is important that I quote her discussion of history at length:

> The fundamental factor that underlies the opposition between the metaphysical Budd/Claggart conflict on the one hand and the reading of Captain Vere on the other can be summed up in a single word: history. While the naive and the ironic readers attempt to impose upon language the functioning of an absolute, timeless universal law (the sign as *either* motivated *or* arbitrary), the question of *martial* law arises within the story precisely to reveal the law as a *historical* phenomenon, to underscore the element of contextual mutability in the conditions of any act of reading. Arbitrariness and motivation, irony and literality, are parameters between which language constantly fluctuates, but only historical context determines which proportion of each is perceptible to each reader. Melville indeed shows history to be a story not only of events but also of fluctuations in the very functioning of irony and belief:

The event *converted into irony for a time* those spirited strains of Dibdin. . . . [*BB*, p. 22]

Everything is *for a term venerated* in navies. [*BB*, p. 135]

The opposing critical judgments of Vere's decision to hang Billy are divided, in the final analysis, according to the place they attribute to history in the process of justification. For the ironists, Vere is misusing history for his own self-preservation or for the preservation of a world safe for aristocracy. For those who accept Vere's verdict as tragic but necessary, it is Melville who has stacked the historical cards in Vere's favor. In both cases, the conception of history as an interpretive instrument remains the same: it is its *use* that is being judged. And the very fact that *Billy Budd* criticism itself historically moves from acceptance to irony is no doubt itself interpretable in the same historical terms. [Pp. 590–91]

History, it would seem, does limit the play of language at any moment in time. A particular set of historical circumstances conditions any reading—including Johnson's. The narrator's comment on how Dibdin's line, "*And as for my life, 'tis the King's!*", can be converted by historical events into irony even seems to anticipate critics' ironic reading of the line " 'God Bless Captain Vere' " (*BB*, p. 124), which Billy delivers "in the clear melody of a singing-bird." Billy, like Dibdin, can compose his own songs and as a songwriter is "no mean auxiliary to the English government at that European conjuncture" (*BB*, p. 22). When this flawed Orpheus finally sings out to support Vere, he emits lines that the events of history can transform into irony.

But to admit the historical conditioning of an act of reading is not, according to Johnson, to offer a ground for judgment. Because history is inaccessible to us except in textual or narrative form, to appeal to history seems to be no more than an appeal to another text. Before we can *use* history to judge, we have to interpret history from texts. Rather than grounding the endless series of ironies involved in judgment, an appeal to history adds to it. As Johnson summarizes: "the exact signifying value of history" remains suspended. "Judgment, then, would seem to ground itself in a suspension of the opposition between textuality and referentiality, just as politics can be seen as that which makes it impossible to draw a line between 'language' and 'life' " (p. 595).

I would agree that in using interpretations of history to support our individual judgments we turn "history" into a text. But

I would add that even if individual readings (including mine) *use* history in this way, it does not follow that history is textual. History, while inaccessible to us except through texts, is not merely another text. History is not the boggy ground of what-might-have-been; history is what was and is. To quote Fredric Jameson, history "is precisely not given as representation but rather as an *absent cause,* as that which can never know full representaton."[26] History occupies the gap between textuality and representation that Johnson calls our suspended ground for judgment. It is my contention that in writing *Billy Budd* Melville creates a situation in which not Vere but history becomes his spokesman, a situation in which history can judge both the book's actions as well as our judgments of those actions.

According to traditional views, the proper way to allow history to speak is to produce a reading that reads a text according to the conditions of the times.[27] In terms of *Billy Budd* this would mean that we should judge Captain Vere according to the standards of his age, not ours. Indeed, the narrator seems to support the necessity of such a "historical" interpretation.

> Says a writer whom few know, "Forty years after a battle it is easy for a non-combatant to reason about how it ought to have been fought. It is another thing personally and under fire to direct the fighting while involved in the obscuring smoke of it. Much so with respect to other emergencies involving considerations both practical and moral, and when it is imperative promptly to act. The greater the fog the more it imperils the steamer, and speed is put on though at the hazard of running somebody down. Little ween the snug card-players in the cabin of the responsibilities of the sleepless man on the bridge." [*BB,* p. 110]

The implication: a reader should not use hindsight to judge Captain Vere, but should instead thrust himself into Vere's foggy position.

The point, however, is that in writing *Billy Budd* Melville creates a situation to help clear the fog by giving us the privilege of hindsight. The "action" of *Billy Budd* takes place almost one hundred years prior to Melville's act of writing. Melville and his reader are in the position to judge Vere's judgment according to the direction history has taken. When we do so, Vere's judgment seems clearly to support a dead order, a soon-to-be-abandoned system of repressive naval discipline, a soon-to-be-abandoned system of control by a king rather than a parliament. Is the reader's role to blind himself to the hindsight that history affords him, or is it to use his present position in history to help him judge? Put another way, when a reader acknowledges that he inevitably judges from the standpoint of the present, doesn't he also acknowledge that history plays a role in his judgment?

What needs to be emphasized is that the traditional "histor-·ical" way of reading is actually ahistorical. Those who believe that to produce a historical reading is to reconstruct the perspective of the past which allows us to discover a textual meaning that remains fixed over time actually lead to a denial of history, since a reader like Johnson can easily prove that any knowledge of "the existing conditions of the past" is textual knowledge. To read historically is not to deny our present perspective but to acknowledge that any judgment of a text is grounded in the present. Rather than closing us off from the past, our present perspective, because it is a product of the past, gives us access to it. Such an attitude does not lead to a tyranny of the present because, if we reflect on our judgments of the past, we can expose the presuppositions of our present age and realize that our actions and judgments will be judged by the future.[28] E. D. Hirsch's hermeneutic of a past meaning and a present significance is replaced by Robert Weimann's of a past significance and a present meaning.[29]

In *Billy Budd* Melville is able to show that events of the past have significance precisely because they have a present meaning. His method is not, as some might argue, to offer a fictional account of past events that is "truer" than the fictional account recorded in "objective" histories; his "inside narrative" undercuts any claim it makes fully to represent the past. Instead Melville gives us the opportunity to examine events as they might have been. The radical thrust of his account of what might have been is to offer a supplement to the authorized view of history not "readily to be found in the libraries" (*BB*, p. 23). In doing so he exposes one of the biggest risks involved in reducing history to mere textuality: the risk of denying past events significance for the present, the corollary of which is denying present events significance for the future. It is the reduction of history to textuality that allows "states everywhere, including America" to shade events like the Great Mutiny "off into the historical background. Such events can not be ignored, but there is a considerate way of historically treating them" (*BB*, p. 23). While the authorized version of history attempts to consign certain events to silence, Melville's unauthorized text calls attention to the silences that most of our lives fall into and shows the consequences of the choice of silence. As Walter Benjamin writes, "only that historian will have the gift of fanning the spark of hope in the past who is firmly convinced that *even the dead* will not be safe from the enemy if he wins. And this enemy has not ceased to be victorious."[30]

Furthermore, it should not be forgotten that one relatively certain event from the past that Melville's text records is his own writing of it. It is a significant event because it produces a text that, as a product of the past recreating the might-have-been of a more distant past, exists in the present to speak to us and judge our actions and judgments which will shape the future.

Of course, to appeal to history as a grounds for judgment is not to insure a fixed reading of *Billy Budd*. At no historical moment will the social conditions be such as to guarantee that every reader will agree with a particular reading of a text. The reading of *Billy Budd* might have moved from acceptance to irony over time, but at no time has there been universal agreement. Further, history itself is always changing. When we make judgments of a text we, like Vere, cannot help but judge according to the historical circumstances we are in. While we have the advantage of hindsight to judge Vere, like Vere, when we judge we are influenced by the inherited ideologies (and ways of reading) of our time. With hindsight the next reader or generation of readers can expose our errors. But what gives that reader or generation of readers the advantage of hindsight remains history. In other words, while the awareness of the historicity of every act of reading does not insure a fixed reading of a text, it does expose the myth of believing in a realm outside of history in which a text's language has totally free (and innocent) play, a realm that can be appealed to to label all readings within history equally partial. Johnson's reading is as ahistorical as those which she deconstructs.

Melville's text does not deny the problematics of judgment; in fact, as Johnson's reading better than any other shows, it reveals them. Johnson is nowhere more acute than when she remarks that the essence of a judgment is that it is open to future judgments. Thus, in adopting a strategy of reading that does not judge, Johnson refuses to engage the very problematics of political judgment that she has described. Although she claims that "it is judging, not murderng, that Melville is asking us to judge" (p. 592), Johnson admits that Vere's position in a structure of power allows his judgment to become an act of murder. That action cries out for judgment calling for more action calling for more judgment and so on in a continual process of history. By not judging Johnson tries to escape from the process of history as judgment and action, an escape accomplished by retreating into an ahistorical realm of textuality. The escape into textuality leads Johnson to make statements like the following: "This is why Melville's choice of historical setting is so significant: the war between France and England at the time of the French Revolution is as striking an example of the simultaneous functioning of differences within and between as is the confrontation between Billy and Claggart in relation to their own internal differences. War, indeed, is the absolute transformation of *all* differences into *binary* differences" (p. 596).

I would argue that Melville's choice of historical setting has a more important significance. Although our knowledge of it will always be textual, the war following the French Revolution is as striking an example as we have of an event in the past that caused changes still felt in the present. This would seem to be the lesson we could glean from a passage that, if we were to rely on accepted textual authority, would not be given the privileged status of inclusion in the definitive reading text of *Billy Budd* Johnson uses, even though it once had authorization to serve as the book's preface.[31]

The year 1797, the year of this narrative, belongs to a period which, as every thinker now feels, involved a crisis for Christendom not exceeded in its undetermined momentousness at the time by any other era whereof there is record. The opening proposition made by the Spirit of that Age involved the rectification of the Old World's hereditary wrongs. In France, to some extent, this was bloodily effected. But what then? Straightway the Revolution regency as righter of wrongs itself became a wrongdoer, one more oppressive than the Kings. Under Napoleon it enthroned upstart kings, and initiated that prolonged agony of Continental war whose final throe was at Waterloo. During those years not the wisest could have foreseen that the outcome of all would be what to some thinkers apparently it has since turned out to be, a political advance along nearly the whole line for Europeans.

Now, as elsewhere hinted, it was something caught from the

Revolutionary Spirit that at Spithead emboldened the man-of-war's
men to rise against real abuses, long-standing ones, and afterwards
at the Nore to make inordinate and aggressive demands, successful
resistance to which was confirmed only when the ringleaders were
hung for an admonitory spectacle to the anchored fleet. Yet in a
way analogous to the operation of the Revolution at large, the Great
Mutiny, though by Englishmen naturally deemed monstrous at the
time, doubtless gave the first latent prompting to most important
reforms in the British navy. [*BB*, pp. 97–98]

If we read this passage as one of those ragged edges that
Melville could not weave into his narrative, we can see why he
felt it important enough not to silence it by crossing it out as he
had other passages. In a short view of history, the revolutionary
spirit seems to lead to no more than a repetition of the wrongs
it tries to replace, just as the versions of truth that Melville's
subversive fictions offer to replace the authorized version succumb to their own critique. But, in a long view, the revolutionary spirit is effective; by risking error and the judgment of
history, it probably leads to important reforms.

To escape the responsibility of judging by having all foundation for judgment disappear into texts is to risk submitting to
the system of authority that controls which passages are included in the reading text we call history. It is to risk accepting
a system in which some linguistic possibilities may never be
allowed to play because they have been silenced at the level of
production. Furthermore, it is to deny an important function
of literature, which is not only to represent man's condition in
the world as it is but, through providing a glimpse of what
might be, to help change man's condition in the world by making us see that our view of "what is" is conditioned by inherited
ways of reading. To deny this function of literature is to be like
Captain Vere, who carefully selects texts to confirm his convictions, convictions that he could not confirm by turning to society; it is these convictions that act as "a dyke against those
invading waters of *novel* opinion, social, political and otherwise"
(*BB*, p. 36, my emphasis) coming from France.

Similarly, J. Hillis Miller defends deconstruction's selection
of texts from the traditional canon because the texts it selects
support deconstruction's conviction that man's "situation in relation to language" or "the human condition generally" will not
be affected by a "change in the material base or in the class
structure," that, in fact, a determining material base is but "one

element in the traditional metaphysical system [deconstruction] wants to put in question."[32]

More sophisticated than Vere, deconstructive critics like Johnson and Miller do not claim directly to know the way it is. Instead they claim that the way it is is that we will never know the way it is. Man's "situation in relation to language" inevitably results in gaps *within* cognition. To be sure, it would be naive to argue that we can eliminate the gaps within cognition and the gaps between action and knowing that, as Johnson shows so convincingly, make politics problematic. At the same time, it is not naive to argue that the action of *Billy Budd* shows that certain political structures contribute to creating more gaps. If Billy's speech defect is a natural condition, his gaps of silence are forced upon him by a repressive political system that exploits his desire to appear innocent. Nor is it naive to point out that rather than working to overcome the problematics of politics, Johnson's way of reading helps to maintain them. Having recognized the inevitability of gaps within cognition and between knowledge and action, Johnson proves her point by adopting a strategy that refuses to risk closing the gap between knowledge and action by judging Captain Vere. Recognition of the way things are leads to a strategy of reading that perpetuates the way things are.

The deconstructive strategy that is so subversive for traditional students of literature turns out to betray a conservative ideology.[33] Although in a society that places so much stock in textual authority deconstruction has a radical potential, that potential is limited because the world deconstruction subverts is limited. The only authority deconstruction undercuts is textual authority. John Brenkman states this point very clearly.

> The deconstructed system remains a purely philosophical one. This indefinite broadening of history into the area of metaphysics, accompanied by the narrowing of the general text, hides the evasion of all historical specificity; such a strategy has a special appeal precisely because it allows the act of radical critique to withdraw from its actual historical, political, and institutional context. The active neutralization that is so central to deconstructive reading becomes the neutrality of deconstruction itself; the subject who deconstructs is strangely at peace with the work of criticism and negation.[34]

Brenkman might have added that deconstruction can be explained in terms of the historical specificity it seeks to evade. It can be seen as the last-ditch effort of members of a profession, whose role it is to interpret texts, to conserve their position of authority in respect to society. Their method is the ideological one of trying to make their sectional interests appear to be universal ones. More acutely aware than "traditional" humanists that society at large no longer grants the texts they study privileged authority, advocates of deconstruction answer this challenge by demonstrating the groundlessness of all claims to authority. By turning society, history, and nature into texts, they show that their loss of authority is not unique; social, political, and natural authority succumb to the same critique. Having denied all claims to legitimate authority, they are in a position to reclaim the traditional humanist's role in society. Because they are such close readers of texts and because all of civilization is one gigantic text, they, like Captain Vere, claim to be the most sensitive interpreters of man's fate.

It has been my aim in this essay to use the encounter between deconstruction and *Billy Budd* to show that deconstruction's strategy of a closer than close reading is not enough. Rather than giving a more sensitive reading of man's fate, deconstruction works to seal man's fate by confining man to an ahistorical, textual world. Man becomes truly impressed. The ragged edges of *Billy Budd* do not disappear into textuality; they lead outward into history, the realm in which the reader lives and must judge. The text of *Billy Budd* deconstructs the ground of its own textual authority not to render the reader silent but to appeal for a judgment.[35] It is through our acts of judgment that the text of *Billy Budd* in turn judges us. What the encounter of *Billy Budd* with deconstruction shows is that to adopt a judgment of silence is to reveal a conservative ideology, for, as the execution of Billy Budd makes clear, to defer a judgment is ultimately to defer to the existing system of authority.

1. Most recent attempts to go beyond Georg Lukács's ideological studies adhere to this model. Louis Althusser claims that "What art makes us *see* . . . is the *ideology* from which it is born." *Lenin and Philosophy and Other Essays* (London: New Left Books, 1971), p. 204. See also Terry Eagleton, *Criticism and Ideology* (London: New Left Books, 1976), pp. 64–101.

2. See Hayden White's discussion in "Literature and Social Action: Reflections on the Reflection Theory of Literary Art," *New Literary History* 11 (Winter 1980):363–80.

3. This formulation owes much to the work of Hans Robert Jauss.

4. Anthony Giddens, *Central Problems in Social Theory* (Berkeley: University of California Press, 1979), p. 6.

5. Barbara Johnson, "Melville's Fist: The Execution of *Billy Budd*," *Studies in Romanticism* 18 (Winter 1979):567–99. Further references to this essay will be cited in the text. This is a special issue entitled *The Rhetoric of Romanticism* edited by Paul de Man. De Man writes of these essays: "Close reading and rhetorical analysis are eminently teachable and it is a common and productive gesture of all of these papers to outdo the closeness of reading that has been held up to them and to show, by reading the close readings more closely, that they were not nearly close enough" (p. 498). Johnson's essay is included in her book *The Critical Difference: Essays in the Contemporary Rhetoric of Reading* (Baltimore, Md.: Johns Hopkins University Press, 1981).

6. Charles A. Reich, "The Tragedy of Justice in *Billy Budd*," *Yale Review* 56 (1967):368–89. Further references to this essay will be cited in the text.

7. Herman Melville, *Billy Budd*, ed. Milton R. Stern (Indianapolis, Ind.: Bobbs-Merrill, 1975), p. 131. I choose Stern's edition rather than that of Hayford and Sealts because I agree with his editorial decision to be inclusive rather than exclusive. All page references to *Billy Budd* are for this edition, hereafter cited in the text as *BB*.

8. Critics before Johnson seem to ignore the possibility that a text proclaiming that "truth uncompromisingly told will always have its ragged edges" places a critic trying to come up with a consistent reading in an awkward position.

9. See Michael Ryan, "Self-Evidence," *Diacritics* 10 (Summer 1980):2–16, for an attempt to align deconstruction and Marxism.

10. Giddens, *Central Problems in Social Theory*, p. 197.

11. See Max Weber, *The Theory of Social and Economic Organization*, trans. A. M. Henderson and Talcott Parsons (New York: Free Press, 1947), p. 328.

12. Quoted by Jürgen Habermas in *Legitimation Crisis*, trans. Thomas McCarthy (Boston: Beacon Press, 1975), p. 97.

13. Habermas, *Legitimation Crisis*, pp. 97–98.

14. Douglas Hay, "Property, Authority and the Criminal Law," in *Albion's Fatal Tree*, ed. Hay et al. (London: Allen Lane, 1975), pp. 37 and 48.

15. See Charles Mitchell, "Melville and the Spurious Truth of Legalism," *Centennial Review* 12 (1968):110–26.

16. Edgar A. Dryden, *Melville's Thematics of Form* (Baltimore, Md.: Johns Hopkins University Press, 1968), p. 215. Further references to this book will be cited in the text.

17. Phil Withim, *"Billy Budd:* Testament of Resistance," *Modern Language Quarterly* 20 (1959):115–27, points out the applicability of this passage on insanity to Vere.

18. James E. Miller, Jr., *"Billy Budd:* The Catastrophe of Innocence," *Modern Language Notes* 73 (1958):168–76.

19. See Walter L. Reed's argument in "The Measured Forms of Captain Vere," *Modern Fiction Studies* 23 (Summer 1977):227–35.

20. Reich, intent on defending Billy's innocence, argues this point most strongly.

21. Herman Melville, *Moby Dick*, ed. Charles Feidelson, Jr. (Indianapolis, Ind.: Bobbs-Merrill Co., 1964), p. 222.

22. Any discussion of the ideology of silence in Melville's works cannot ignore Bartleby. The silence that follows Bartleby's "I would prefer not to" obviously does not give assent to the ruling system in the same manner that Billy's silence does. Not able to use writing to say "No, in thunder," because he must copy the already existing linguistic codes of his culture, Bartleby decides to say "No" in silence. But that silence is imprisoning and ultimately leads to an ineffectual death. The alternative seems to be to find

some way to use writing not to copy what exists but to create "novel opinions" (*BB*, p. 36), which once again say "No, in thunder."

23. Joseph Schiffman, "Melville's Final Stage, Irony: A Reexamination of *Billy Budd* Criticism," *American Literature* 22 (1950):133, also points out that Billy is no spokesman.

24. See Dryden, Reed, Peter A. Obuchowski, "*Billy Budd* and the Failure of Art," *Studies in Short Fiction* 15 (Fall 1978):445–52, and Nina Baym, "Melville's Quarrel with Fiction," *PMLA* 94 (October 1979):909–23. We should not forget that Melville continued to write poetry during these years, but his silence in his chosen public mode of presentation—prose fiction—does seem significant.

25. Habermas most thoroughly develops these notions. See especially Habermas and Niklas Luhmann, "Vorbereitende Bemerkung zu einer Theorie der kommunikativen Kompetenz," in *Theorie der Gesellschaft oder Sozialtechnologie?* (Frankfurt: Suhrkamp, 1971), pp. 101–41.

26. Fredric Jameson, "Marxism and Historicism," *New Literary History* 11 (Autumn 1979):42. Jameson's essay is essential reading for anyone interested in developing "a properly Marxist *hermeneutic*."

27. In recent years the work of E. D. Hirsch, Jr., has most often been associated with this view. See *Validity in Interpretation* (New Haven, Conn.: Yale University Press, 1967).

28. I rely here on the work of Hans Georg Gadamer in *Truth and Method*, trans. Garrett Barden and John Cumming (New York: Seabury Press, 1975).

29. Robert Weimann, "Past Significance and Present Meaning in Literary History," in *New Directions in Literary History*, ed. Ralph Cohen (Baltimore, Md.: Johns Hopkins University Press, 1974), pp. 43–62. Also see Weimann's "Erzählsituation und Romantypus: Zu Theorie und Genesis realistischer Erzälformen," *Sinn und Form* 18 (1966). In *The Historical Novel*, trans. Hannah and Stanley Mitchell (London: New Left Books, 1962), Georg Lukács argues, "without a felt relationship to the present, a portrayal of history is impossible" (p. 53). In *Versions of the Past* (New York: Oxford University Press, 1974), pp. 157–74, Harry B. Henderson III offers "*Billy Budd:* The Problem of Historical Judgment."

30. Walter Benjamin, "Theses on the Philosophy of History," in *Illuminations*, trans. Harry Zohn (New York: Schocken Books, 1969), p. 255.

31. See Stern's discussion of this passage (*BB*, pp. 149–60).

32. J. Hillis Miller, "Theory and Practice: Response to Vincent Leitch," *Critical Inquiry* 6 (Summer 1980):612.

33. Miller admits deconstruction's conservatism in "Theory and Practice." This has been pointed out by Maria Ruegg, "The End(s) of French Style: Structuralism and Post-Structuralism in the American Context," *Criticism* 21 (Summer 1979):189–216; William E. Cain, "Deconstruction in America: The Recent Literary Criticism of J. Hillis Miller," *College English* 41 (December 1979):367–82; Vincent B. Leitch, "The Lateral Dance: The Deconstructive Criticism of J. Hillis Miller," *Critical Inquiry* 6 (Summer 1980):593–608.

34. John Brenkman, "Deconstruction and the Social Text," *Social Text* 1 (Winter 1979):188.

35. See Ruegg's acute comment: "Making value judgments is precisely the *function* of criticism. And if critics continue to write criticism, in spite of a 'crisis' which would logically reduce them to silence, it is because the function of criticism—that is, of making value judgments about some 'reality' (social, historical, literary)—is a necessary function of any society" ("The End[s] of French Style," p. 216).

Ideology as Narrative: Critical Approaches to *Robinson Crusoe*

Stephen Zelnick

Temple University

T HE term *ideology* has a complex history, and very different concepts gather around it. Even within the Marxist tradition there are at least three divergent definitions: (1) for Marx and Engels in *The German Ideology* ideology is illusory and false thinking, an inversion by which ideas assume an autonomy separate from the historical life process; (2) the later Marx of *Contribution to the Critique of Political Philosophy* requires a distinction between "the material transformation of the economic conditions of production" and the forms of "legal, political, religious, aesthetic or philosophic" practices "where people become conscious of this conflict and fight it out"; and (3) Lenin discusses ideology as a class-bound system of ideas, a theoretical practice, where a revolutionary proletarian ideology does battle with a bourgeois one.[1] In common contemporary parlance *ideology* is a negative term, denoting empty if not fraudulent abstraction that must be corrected by immediate experience or an instrumental philosophy.

All but the second of these concepts, that of the later Marx, agree that ideology is a false, or in Lenin's case, a convenient construct. They also share the view that ideology is separate from practical consciousness, a tabulation of discursive propositions imposed upon consciousness. The mature Marx, however, argues that ideology is inescapable, a constitutive representation of what otherwise cannot be known in itself. It is this positive concept of ideology that is the most useful for a discussion of literature and literary critical practice.

Louis Althusser, in *For Marx,* has developed the fullest discussion of this positive concept. Althusser argues that "ideology is a system (with its own logic and rigour) of representations (images, myths, ideas or concepts, depending on the case)" and, further, that "ideology is as such an organic part of every social totality." Far from being "an aberration or a contingent excrescence of History: it is a structure essential to the historical life of societies." Rather than being made up of discursive statements held at a philosophical distance, "ideology is a system of representations" by which human beings become aware of the "*lived* relation between men and their world." Further, "in ideology men do indeed express, not the relation between them and their conditions of existence, but *the way* they live the relation between them and their conditions of existence: this presupposes both a real relation and an 'imaginary,' 'lived' relation." Finally, "in ideology the real relation is inevitably invested in the imaginary relation, a relation that expresses a *will* (conservative, conformist, reformist, or revolutionary), a hope or a nostalgia, rather than describing a reality."[2]

The implications of this integrated concept for literary study are profound. It argues that the traditional Marxist critical project of demystification mistakes its object. The base/superstructure model looks at literature as illusory, a false account of the relations of production: literature is to be tutored by political economy as if literature were not in itself a form of knowledge otherwise unavailable. Another approach sets out to test a literary work against an abstract set of propositions (e.g., statements concerning individualism/collectivism, competition/cooperation, sexism/feminism, etc.). Since such a test already knows the right answers, nothing will be learned except how well the literary work conforms to some standard of correctness. A still more abstract approach attempts to measure the work by the form of thinking ascribed to a particular epoch. Here, too, what is known precedes what literature has to say about the imaginative strategies by which people live their relation to the real. Such abstract explanations interrupt the special knowledge literature can divulge.

Althusser's comment recommends looking for ideology in literature not as the embodiment of general propositions but in fictional forms, such technical matters as point of view, the strategic shape of narrative, the clash of styles, etc.; in short, in those formal matters which give us access to the underlying, preconscious grid that shapes experience as if by reflex. What can already be identified as ideology has no force: what must be studied instead is what seems most reasonable, natural, and obvious.

In the following discussion I want first to explore three familiar critical practices to understand the consequences of their concept of ideology. The text is *Robinson Crusoe,* and the three critical approaches are: (1) Ian Watt's generally Marxian analysis; (2) J. Paul Hunter's and George A. Starr's source studies; and (3) the recent phenomenological and existentialist approaches of John Richetti and Everett Zimmerman. Next I will look at Defoe's economic writings to identify the contradictions he was working through there and, most important, the force of narrative strategies in a nonliterary setting. Finally, I will discuss *Robinson Crusoe* to understand the ideological maneuvers worked out in a fully fictional narrative.

I take the view that ideology is constructed as a permissive narrative, i.e., a narrative that allows for the management of contradictions to provide a sense of mastery over experience. Rather than being a set of discursive statements, ideology is best understood as a complex discourse extended through a narrative, or, more simply, a way of telling a story. My argument is that people are always busy shaping stories or responding to them within the transparent repertoire of social fictions and that these narratives are busy constructing the best case imaginable for mastering experience and realizing desire. Such narratives make available to people a process for bypassing contradictions through condensation and displacement, repetition with variations, and the eruption of new possibilities. In this deep but not obvious way, ideology is always at work constructing images of one's relation to the real. Literary works put this private experience on display as social systems and are, in fact, the most complete representations of these systems available to us.[3]

The concept of ideology is a central question for literary criticism. So long as ideology is conceived of as separate from the strategies of narrative, the ideological working of literature will be misunderstood; in its place will emerge a view of literary practice as either the direct incorporation of ideas or as a performance totally free from the repertoire of social fictions. Either the literary work will seem determined by abstractions or fully free from them. In both instances the specific knowledge literature makes available, the formation of narratives within powerful social fictions, will be overlooked.

Ian Watt's "*Robinson Crusoe* as Myth" (1951) sees Defoe's novel as having produced one of "the great myths of our civilization," expressing "some of the enduring traits of our social and economic history."[4] However, for Watt the relation of the myth to these enduring traits (an abstracted form of ideology) is complex. In some instances the "Robinson Crusoe" myth is a straightforward celebration of capitalist values, i.e., of individualism, of the restless transformation of nature, of the power of abstract rationality and economic calculation, and of the suppression of emotion. In other modes, the relation is critical and utopian, i.e., the desire for the return to nature, for a simple artisanal production process, and for an escape from the increasingly complex division of labor. In Watt's account, Defoe glorifies emergent capitalism but only by withdrawing production from the complexities of capitalist society. In this way, *Robinson Crusoe* is a wish fulfillment in which "Crusoe's 'island of despair' . . . is actually a utopia," and where "the use of Crusoe as an example [of capitalist ideology] . . . distracts attention from the realities of the economic system as it is."[5]

Watt explains that *homo economicus* is the real hero but that his ugly features—slavery, the subjection of sensuality to rational calculation, the "stolid and inhibited self-sufficiency of Crusoe's outrageous ego-centrism," and his humorless acquisitiveness—have been obscured by Defoe's utopian representation.[6] Yet, according to Watt, the Crusoe myth actually runs counter to the hard ethic of acquisition:

> This may seem surprising, since Defoe, the complacent apologist of nascent industrial capitalism, certainly approved of the new ideology. But as a writer his eye was so keenly on the object, and second thoughts so rarely checked the flow of his pen, that he reported, not his wishes, but the plausible image of the moment, what he knew people would actually do. So it is that he tells us much which, if analyzed, questions not only the simple message of the myth, but even some of his own cherished beliefs.[7] ·

This comment is wonderfully revealing. It shows that for

Watt *Robinson Crusoe* has three levels: (1) the "cherished beliefs" (ideology), Defoe's presumed commitment to a set of propositions; (2) the utopian representation by which the hard edge of those propositions is smoothed over; and (3) the truth of experience, which eludes both ideology and the utopian displacement. Watt proposes a sophisticated reading of the myth to emphasize its instability and a kind of frantic special pleading. Nevertheless, the concept of ideology as a belief system rather than as an all-encompassing narrative system severely weakens Watt's analysis.

First, the belief system Watt ascribes to Defoe is mistaken. As we shall see from Defoe's economic writings, he never was a "complacent apologist of nascent industrial capitalism" (whatever that might have meant in 1719). More important, the ascription precedes the narrative and is based on nothing more than a myth of a unified epochal world view. Second, the notion that the belief system and the utopian displacement are separable leads away from an understanding of how an ideological narrative is formed. Ideological thinking requires a utopian element—there is no separable body of propositions—and it is the narrative that reveals the strategies of displacement. Indeed, Watt's conception of ideology leads him away from narrative to consider instead the detached myth. Finally, the view that there is a representation of experience apart from ideological shaping, produced when the writer's "eye was so keenly on the object," leads Watt to a simple empiricism where facts speak for themselves. Somehow, Watt is arguing, we can scrape off the belief system and the utopian displacement, and the myth will show us experience just as it is.

The one-dimensionality of Watt's concept of ideology is accentuated in his discussion of religion. Since Watt already knows that Defoe's ideology has to do exclusively with economics, religion and all other systems of hope and desire are simply pushed into another category. The idea that ideology might have a "both this—and that" structure and indeed must aspire to a global totality in the hope of encompassing contradictions is unthinkable to Watt's single-dimension ideology.

A subsequent account of *Robinson Crusoe* counters Watt by stressing the importance of Defoe's narrative models. Watt pays scant attention to the actual narrative of *Robinson Crusoe* or to the field of texts out of which Defoe's novel emerged. J. Paul Hunter's *The Reluctant Pilgrim* and George A. Starr's *Defoe and*

Spiritual Autobiography locate Defoe's novel within a tradition that helps explain its narrative structure.[8] Hunter and Starr resist a strategic reading of the narrative, but they do relate *Robinson Crusoe* to the textual traditions that allowed it to appear. They note that Defoe's novel is performed on a stage already constructed not only by travel narratives but by Puritan guide-books and spiritual autobiographies. The disobedience to a parent's wise teaching, the restless wandering that ensues, the confusion and loss of personal effectiveness, the warnings sent by a tutoring God, the series of half-hearted and merely convenient repentances, a deepening sense of sinfulness, further miraculous signs of Providence, the true conversion, the regaining of power over the self and external forces, the steady deepening of faith and power—this pattern, along with familiar metaphors of voyages, shipwreck, and the parable of the Prodigal Son, certainly indicate in profusion a definite textual tradition for *Robinson Crusoe*.

Where Hunter and Starr go wrong is in absorbing *Robinson Crusoe* back into that tradition, as if by working these traditional materials into a novel Defoe had not changed everything. In order to claim *Robinson Crusoe* for the ideological position of its sources, Hunter and Starr argue that Defoe merely expanded the dramatized examples that illustrate doctrinal points in the guide-books and autobiographies: the movement from tract to novel is merely quantitative. Hunter and Starr do notice the contradictions that litter Defoe's novel (notably that Crusoe's sin leads all too conveniently to an immense fortune), but in their efforts to construct a harmonized ideology they portray this contradiction as a "dialectical" relation between spirituality and its secular embodiment: the shifts between religion and secular concerns are portrayed as the psychological realism of an unsteady state of redemption. In this view the economic dimension is easily absorbed into the religious emphasis of Defoe's models. However, as we shall see, Defoe's novel actually devours these earlier texts and uses them parodically to mark their limitations when measured against a full, realistic narrative.

Contemporary criticism has continued to employ a rigid concept of ideology but with the further purpose of rejecting the importance of ideology in literature absolutely. John J. Richetti, in *Defoe's Narratives: Situations and Structures,* argues against both previous positions: Richetti claims that

the historian of ideas who extrapolates themes out of Defoe's narratives as their ultimate content is in danger of ignoring at his peril
the truism that story-telling is by its nature something different
from discursive statement, something dynamic and relational in
which discursive statement plays only a role, and a role in which it is
often transformed into something quite unlike itself.[9]

The work of the novel, in Richetti's view, is to nullify ideology
by pressing discursive statements against the abrasive wheel of
unmediated experience. Crusoe is

> realized as a character in the conflict in him between two historical
> factors: the expansive ideology of capitalism and the conservative
> moral and religious ideology which is its logical opposite. His posi-
> tion as a consciousness aware of the claims of those ideologies liber-
> ates him from them.[10]

Whatever his commitments otherwise, the novelist is committed
"*qua* novelist first and simply to the revelation of that process
whereby experience is separated from ideology and becomes
conscious of itself as the powerful if often undirected opposite
of ideology."[11]

A similar strategy is enacted by Everett Zimmerman in *Defoe
and the Novel.* In Zimmerman's account, "Defoe's characters try
to find spiritual meaning, but the material of their lives is ex-
tremely stubborn. Defoe's novels reveal the discordancies of
mind that result from a life having only a dubious relationship
either to an inner principle or to a stable external one."[12] This
existential Crusoe is only "unremitting activity": Defoe "surrounds Crusoe with fragments of meaning; the bare character
is chaotic energy. Crusoe is the forms he adopts only for as long
as he adopts them."[13] For Zimmerman as for Richetti, the novel
opens up a free territory where experience breaks loose from
any shaping force and the chaos of life supersedes the authority
of dogma.

This argument makes sense as a reaction against Watt and
against Hunter and Starr. Watt is already on the edge of this
view anyhow, since in his account Defoe's ideology is overwhelmed when he works out his novel. Hunter and Starr
rigidify narrative tradition to the point where any adaptation of
it is quickly absorbed back into the convention. Richetti and
Zimmerman, then, turn the tables on this restrictive notion by
asserting the novel's absolute freedom from any sort of determination. Their concept of ideology remains the same; only
they argue that ideology has no place in fiction at all.

But this concept of ideology as a set of discursive statements is a phantom. For ideology shapes the narrative structure at all levels and shapes the relation between static propositions and the efforts to elude them. Ideology, in the novel as in the living fictions in the minds of everyday people, is a structure of permissive relations that allows both the comforting stability of absolute values and the illusion of rebelliousness and freedom from them; the spiritual transcendence of religion and the acquisitive rampage through the material world; self-centeredness and the sense of communal participation; the full use of other people and the belief in complete service to them, etc. If narrative structures were not flexible enough to provide this plenitude of allowances, they would be discarded as barriers to our wishes.

Chasing off the mere phantom of ideology only leaves the real expression of ideology (that grid of preconscious assumptions that shapes the relation of contradictions in a narrative) unexplained. The view that inconsistencies in the narrative cause it to disintegrate into discrete moments (Zimmerman) is a refusal to see how ideology always operates to permit conflicting elements to form a convenient unity. The denial of contradiction and of the effort to achieve the illusion of an immediate and seamless unity is, finally, itself always an attempt to claim an unmediated unity between empirically observed experience and idealist universals: i.e., the ultimate ideological illusion that thoughts and actions arise unmotivated and apart from the social-historical moment that generates them.

The problem for Marxist and, indeed, for all other sociologically oriented literary criticism is to construct this social-historical moment so that it does not reduce literature to straightforward reflection or homology. Fortunately, in the case of Defoe, we have another realm of discourse, Defoe's economic writings, to help explain his social outlook and the narratives he arranges to support it. Defoe's economic writings are supported all along the way by brief stories that put on display the imaginative discourse of a class ideology as a series of fictions.

A recent study of these writings, Peter Earle's *The World of Defoe,* reveals Defoe's efforts to construct contradictory values into compelling, though often perplexing, unities through narrative. We learn from Earle, too, how mistaken is Watt's claim that Defoe was a "complacent apologist of nascent industrial capitalism." As a spokesman for the interests of Dissenting tradesmen, a group far from established in either a social or economic sense and leading a precarious political existence, there was little for Defoe to be complacent about. Defoe was fearful of the new forces of productive efficiency and narrow profit rationality; he saw greatly increased production and more efficient distribution and exchange as threats to social stability. Indeed, there is a profoundly conservative strain in Defoe that identifies him with mid-seventeenth-century mercantile theories still defensive about the disruptive tendencies of independent mercantile activity.

Before Adam Smith devised an "invisible hand" to guide the selfish activities of each toward the greatest good for all, middle-class ideologues were far less ready to assert radical individualism as the basis for social order. Smith shaped a fictional unity of opposites in which the practical particular and the idealist general interpenetrate immediately. Defoe negotiated his world picture with a more complex dialectic, where powerful contradictions had to be mediated by a long process not unlike a narrative discourse. In the realm of the novel, these contradictions had to be brought into conformity in what aspired to be an all-encompassing discourse, but we can see this process already at work in Defoe's economic writings.

Defoe often encountered absolutely antagonistic contradictions. Thus, he was committed to increased agricultural production even though the only way surplus grain could be consumed was in the form of gin. In this case, "the moralistic Defoe, who in other writings was to describe drink as the father of all vices, became the champion of the drink trade when he was wearing his economic hat."[14] Another such contradiction was between middle-class habits and aspirations and those of servants. If servants were to adopt the same habits of thrift to raise themselves in the world, not only would they become bad servants, but a great conduit for ready consumption would be constricted with the result of unemployment, bankruptcies, and higher poor rates. As always, class boundaries mark the line where contradictions can be upheld.

Within the confines of his own class activity, however, contra-

dictions had to appear nonantagonistic. A revealing example is
Defoe's argument that the basis of social stability lies in economic inefficiency. Earle summarizes Defoe's case as follows:

> The more remote any centre of production was from London, the
> larger the number of pack-horses and carriers needed to carry the
> year's output and the larger the number of inns fully employed in
> catering for their needs at the end of each day's slow travel. The
> very congestion and physical size of the city was an advantage. How
> many coachmen, porters and carters were necessary to carry people
> and goods from the outskirts of the city or the waterfront to the
> centre? An enormous number, but one that was made even bigger
> by the fact that each one of them could move only slowly in the
> crowded streets.[15]

From a long view, though hardly a disinterested one (the
tradesman's function is the central theme), a circuitous, wandering, indirect path was the only efficient route to economic
stability. The longer the route of transmission, the more stability was guaranteed. Contradictions were to be overcome by an
elaborate narrative.

The sharpest contradiction internal to Defoe's class values
was between means and ends. The emphasis on long, steady
labor, on thrift and sobriety, on energetic daily persistence
through good times and bad, on the careful accumulation of
funds for investment, on the wary attention to inventories,
prices, and profit margins—all these constituted what Defoe
termed "the most noble, most instructive and improving way of
life."[16] The long sustained effort to master a difficult destiny
shaped character to moral seriousness. But the rigors of the
middle station were also the way to achieve the best life of all,
the leisure of a gentleman. In Earle's words: "How could one
preach work to the poor and teach the middle station that every
minute of their time was precious, when the most alluring objective of such a close attention to the main task was to attain the
blissful state of gentility, and hence be idle?"[17] And this was no
mere abstraction since the advance of trade and the expansion
of banking and government finance had made rentier incomes
readily available for tradesmen with capital. Diligent labors and
thrift could now purchase luxurious leisure and extravagant
consumption.

To a view from outside Defoe's class, the tendency of Puritan
thrift to hunger after extravagance and of moral endurance to
give way to sumptuous leisure would seem an occasion for hy-

pocrisy pure and simple. From inside the middle-class view, obviously, this could not be the case, and the strategies by which these contradictions were to be presented as noncontradictory were the major project of middle-class writers. The construction of a narrative that allowed for the desire to accumulate wealth and enjoy the material world while still adhering to a stern and spiritualized morality and, further, constructing one that provided for the middle class the energizing identity of embattled outsiders in the social struggle was the central project of the bourgeois novel.

The work of ideology, then, is to construct a narrative that permits the resolution of contradictions while suppressing the totality of social relations that would deny the special privilege claimed by a class view. Another significant example is Defoe's short narrative on theodicy. After allowing that God could have created a utopia of natural plenty so readily available "that no man need go a mile from home for anything he wanted," Defoe rejected this paradise because, in Earle's words, it "would have meant no hard work and no trade, a state of affairs as unattractive to the Almighty as it was to Defoe." Material plenty had been provided but only in such a way that "materials for clothing, varieties for feeding, and many of the numberless *addenda* to the pleasures and conveniences of life were inaccessible . . . but by labour, industry, and correspondence."[18] A society built on production and, especially, on trade was thereby founded by God's plan, and the sweat of man's brow (particularly the sweat of another's brow, for tradesman do not share Adam's curse quite equally with the "mechanick part of mankind") became the vehicle for constructing humankind in history. This account gives a severe twist to the Biblical tradition, but it allows deprivation and the labor it elicits to become a grander gift (a paradise dispersed, happier far, where the tradesman's function of transportation and distribution becomes the basis not only for a particular society but the central project of human history).

Religion cannot be thought of as separate from social determination, but the religious dimension also cannot be absorbed into economics without losing an understanding of the special force of religion in constructing ideological narratives. When Defoe's religious narratives are placed alongside his economic fictions, the conformity of their patterns becomes obvious. Hunter's emphasis on the importance of the Prodigal Son in

Robinson Crusoe is certainly justified. For Defoe, the discovery of a full relation to God required a wandering off, a getting lost in the shapeless world of random events, an experience of isolation and powerlessness so that the full force of the Father's love could be known as a release from the hopeless bondage of a contradictory and disorienting world. The parable allowed for an absolute ideal but also for imperfection. Going astray was not only inevitable, it was the necessary condition for being found. This appeal to the necessity of error can certainly be portrayed as merely convenient (the "repentance gambit"), but this view denies the narrative strategy Defoe worked to allow a plenitude of options.

Defoe's paradigmatic sketch of the tradesman's life reveals the usefulness of the Prodigal Son parable. Defoe writes:

> To fall is common to all mankind; the fall and rise is a particular that few men arise to, and no man so easy and so often as the tradesman; but to fall into the very dirt of scandal and reproach and rise with reputation; to fall with infamy and rise with applause; to fall detested and rise caressed and embraced by all mankind; this I think is a kind of peculiar to the tradesman [*sic*]; nay, to the unhappy unfortunate tradesman, who by the one turn of his affairs is lifted out of the mire into a station in life, infinitely superior to the best condition he was ever in before.[19]

This is an odd passage, a fiction hovering uneasily between a description of what *has* been, what *might* be, and what *must* be, between the accidents of an actual case and a determinative pattern of experience. As such, it is a fine demonstration of how narrative is busy in Defoe's economic writings. More specifically, it reveals the close symmetry between the parable of the Prodigal Son and the tradesman's program for perseverance. In both cases the narrative is permissive: the long process of wandering and change is anchored in a definite set of ideals that, in turn, supply the vagaries of experience with a fixed point around which to gravitate. It is important to observe, too, that the close symmetry between the two narratives is never collapsed into identity. Defoe's form of ideology requires the autonomy of the religious to provide a special sanction, but the secular realm remains autonomous also. The tradesman's story needs the parable to attain the status of something more than accidental description of what *might* be. The connection must be suppressed so that the account of "the real" is something more than a moralizing tale and, at the same time, is anchored, by slanting association, with a pattern that sanctions what *must* be. This complex passage between the religious and the secular in Defoe must be kept open to permit an understanding of the fully permissive narrative.

A discussion of the narrative of *Robinson Crusoe* might seem to require us to trace the story line of the novel, but in fact that sort of reading, a reading that aims to show how smoothly ordered and harmonious the narrative is, would be totally useless. Instead, we need to find the seams in the fabric, those places where the narrative comes open to give us a glimpse into the special weaving that works to cover over contradictions. Those moments in the text are not hidden; in fact, they are set right before us to reveal/conceal the ideological working that has gone into producing the text. How, after all, can one conceal something without in some way noting its presence, even if this is only a matter of indicating the space where its presence ought to be? The best way into the narrative of *Robinson Crusoe* is to observe those special moments when the text raises the most curious questions about itself, where, to continue my metaphor, knots and snags appear in the fabric. The customary view of these moments is that they reflect Defoe's careless haste in writing *Robinson Crusoe,* but that is no explanation.

Robinson Crusoe opens with a statement of ideals presented as a model for young Crusoe.[20] Father Crusoe expounds a summary wisdom, but it is offered to a young man restless for life experience and, therefore, is an extraordinarily incongruous wisdom. Defoe's text accentuates this incongruity by overplaying the tune of ease and peacefulness in Father Crusoe's words, an emphasis that is meaningless for young Crusoe. At the same time we are being asked to accept the wisdom of this teaching, but merely as an ultimate truth that only time and experience can tell. The novel forces us to see this dry moralizing, characteristic of the religious-moral texts of Defoe's time, as a dead letter that needs to be replaced by the sort of text a novel is. *Robinson Crusoe* begins, then, by marking its difference from traditional texts.

Father Crusoe's speech is a tedious lecture, proscribing the young man's energies by imposing the stale destiny of "a Life of Ease and Pleasure." Defoe depicts Father Crusoe as frail, "confined by the Gout," and inanely repetitious. Defoe means

us to observe an enfeebled wisdom, now safely removed from
the business of the world. "My Father, who was very ancient"
drones on about living the sort of life which will not rob "the
Soul of Peace, and the Body of Rest; not enrag'd with the
Passion of Envy, or secret burning Lust of Ambition for great
things; but in easy Circumstances sliding gently thro' the
World, and sensibly tasting the Sweets of living" (p. 6). The
sermon associates stability with death:

> He told me it was for Men of desperate Fortunes on one Hand,
> or of Aspiring, superior Fortune on the other, who went abroad
> upon Adventures, to rise by Enterprise, and make themselves fa-
> mous in undertakings of a nature out of the common Road; that
> these things were all either too far above me, or too far below me;
> that mine was the middle State, or what might be called the upper
> Station of *Low Life,* which he had found by long Experience was the
> best State in the World, the most suited to human Happiness, not
> exposed to the Miseries and Hardships, the Labour and Sufferings
> of the mechanick Part of Mankind, and not embarass'd with the
> Pride, Luxury, Ambition and Envy of the upper Part of Mankind.
> [Pp. 5–6]

This is the "Way Men went silently and smoothly thro' the
World and comfortably out of it, not embarass'd with the
Labours of the Hands or of the Head" (p. 6).

This wisdom, in its tiresome style, begs to be rejected. And,
indeed, all that Father Crusoe aims to save his son from is
happily accomplished by young Crusoe. Crusoe grasps life
vigorously, learns to work with hands and head, rises in the
world, and even becomes famous. Responding energetically to
the dynamic expansion of colonial empire, Crusoe takes the
next step in a tradesman's historical fortunes. However, Crusoe
also continues to be guided by his father's emphasis on stability
and security, and the novel manages to argue for all these divergent potentials: an easeful life with high adventure, hard
work with the pride of vast property, peace of mind with the
spice of danger, etc. So long as Crusoe can resolve "like a true
repenting Prodigal; to go home to [his] Father," his life adventure has a fixed point to anchor his experience in the world.
The long journey outward will take him home to the wisdom of
his father.

This original contradiction propels the entire narrative.
However, Crusoe's wanderings bring him up against a variety
of specific contradictions the narrative means to resolve. Three

famous moments in the novel—famous because they have baffled the critics—will help us understand how the narrative manages contradictions in a permissive way. These moments are: (1) the sale of the *Maresco,* Xury, into slavery; (2) Crusoe's histrionic speech rejecting money; and (3) Friday's embarrassing interruption of Crusoe's catechism.

When the *Maresco,* Xury, helps him escape his captivity in North Africa, Crusoe promises to make the boy a "great Man" (p. 21), and even "learns to love him ever after" (p. 23). A short time later Crusoe sells him to the Portuguese captain who rescued them. Crusoe reports:

> I was very loath to sell the poor Boy's liberty, who had assisted me so faithfully in procuring my own. However when I let him know my Reason, he [the captain] own'd it to be just and offer'd me this Medium, that he would give the Boy an Obligation to set him free in ten Years, if he turn'd Christian; upon this, and Xury saying he was willing to go to him, I let the Captain have him. [P. 29]

Critics have enjoyed feeling morally superior to Crusoe's treatment of Xury, as if Xury were a real boy whom a real Crusoe had betrayed. They have failed to ask why Xury appears in the novel at all; or, put another way, what problem the appearance of Xury is meant to handle. The Xury incident is certainly not the only case of Crusoe's encountering the "lesser" peoples of the earth and of the problems of slavery—Crusoe is shipwrecked on a voyage to purchase African slaves for his Brazilian plantation, worries his way through the question of the right to murder cannibals, and domesticates the savage Friday. Defoe is addressing a problem that he, as an economist of world trade, recognizes as disturbing and unavoidable. Defoe knew very well why the slave trade was necessary: "the case is as plain as cause and consequence: Mark the climax. No African trade, no negroes; no negroes no sugars, gingers, indicoes etc.; no sugars etc. no islands; no islands no continent; no continent no trade."[21] And one might continue, no trade no tradesmen; no tradesmen no fulfillment of God's plan for constructing morally disciplined and energetic human beings.

The problem is to square the necessity of slavery with the claim for humanity. This is why the Xury incident appears in *Robinson Crusoe,* and why its contradictions must be brought partway to the surface and then be hastily resolved. A compromise ("Medium") is arranged to provide the hope of liberty and is further assured by contract ("Obligation"): this is notably unlike the slavery practiced by the Sallee pirates. Conversion to Christianity offers Xury the chance to join the community of the saved; and, finally, Xury's agreement to the contract is enthusiastic (although he has been consulted rather late in the negotiations). Defoe allowed himself and his readers to believe that slavery could be thought of as a contractual agreement, entered into mutually, and to the benefit of both parties.

To be sure, the argument is massively displaced. Neither Xury nor Friday is a negro. Indeed, Crusoe encounters black Africans along the shoreline without any reference to slavery aside from Crusoe's readiness to call them "my Negroes." Friday is insistently described as not negroid—with a "very good Countenance" that includes "all the Sweetness and Softness of an *European*. . . . His Hair was long and black, not curl'd like Wool. . . . His Face was round, and plump; his Nose small, not flat like the Negroes" (p. 160). And yet the whole problem they refer to *is* African slavery. This dislocation allows Defoe and his readers to understand force as reason, slavery as liberation, and mastery as paternal solicitude. The displacement from the "Negro question" is necessary, for none of these fantastic allowances could very well survive even a fictional account specific to the slave trade.

The usual claim by critics that Crusoe's treatment of Xury is simply hypocritical or another slip of Defoe's hasty pen is inadequate because it cannot account for the appearance of the incident in the first place nor the necessity for allowing this strange contradiction to appear. These moments in *Robinson Crusoe* only make sense as ideological maneuvers aimed to resolve distressing problems in the picture of the real world.

Certainly the most curious moment in *Robinson Crusoe* is when Crusoe discovers a drawer full of coins on board the ship he is stripping:

> I smil'd to my self at the Sight of this Money. O Drug! said I aloud, what art thou good for? Thou art not worth to me, no not the taking off of the Ground; one of those Knives is worth all this Heap; I have no Manner of use for thee, e'en remain where thou art, and go to the Bottom as a Creature whose life is not worth saving. However, upon Second Thoughts, I took it away, and wrapping all this in a Piece of Canvas, I began to think of making another Raft. [P. 47]

Critics have had the devil of a time accounting for this passage. Certainly Defoe could not have produced this passage by inattention to something earlier. The inconsistency, if meant to be merely comic, is not clearly motivated. It does fit a pattern of humor in the novel where an overladen moralism gives way to practicality (as in the rejection of Father Crusoe's sermon or in Crusoe's ludicrous effort to guide Friday through a Sunday-school catechism). However, these moments of humor are not simply comic but instead indicate serious ideological problems. The money speech, an obvious snag in the fabric of the text, leads us to unravel a deep problem that a major portion of the novel aims to resolve.

A passage from Marx's *Grundrisse* identifies the contradiction efficiently:

> The further back we go into history, the more the individual and, therefore, the producing individual seems to depend on and belong to a larger whole; at first it is, quite naturally, the family and the clan, which is but an enlarged family; later on, it is the community growing up in its different forms out of the clash and amalgamation of clans. It is only in the eighteenth century, in "civil society," that the different forms of social union confront the individual as a mere means to his private ends, as an external necessity. But the period in which this view of the isolated individual becomes prevalent is the very one in which the interrelations of society (general from this point of view) have reached the highest state of development.[22]

Marx is describing the ideological fiction that dominates bourgeois political economy, the Robinsonades of Smith and Ricardo. At the very time when society is developing most rapidly into a complex interrelation of productive functions, individualism is being affirmed as absolutely self-sufficient.

Robinson Crusoe was a complex reponse to the growing interrelatedness of Defoe's society. Crusoe's adventure assured readers that each one of them could produce his own life if that were necessary. The independent self was asserted as the true measure of reality, reaching contractual agreements with other freely determined selves, none of them ontologically dependent upon society. But even in the utopian fantasy of Crusoe's island, traces are left of his debt to society and the interrelation of productive functions that produce his life—the tools he scavenges are the most obvious traces, but technical processes (making bread, pots, defensive outworks, etc.; planting; domesticating and herding animals; writing and language; etc.) are hardly Crusoe's own invention, and his structure of faith, supplied with the grand tool of the Bible and the special knowledge of its use, does not emerge directly from nature for Crusoe. Yet, this complex repertoire of resources allowed Crusoe the illusion of self-sufficiency because they were made to seem inert until Crusoe "discovered" them for himself. The necessary illusion is that Crusoe could originate in himself.

As Watt argued, the "Island of Despair" is often a utopian paradise. Crusoe writes:

> Thus I liv'd mighty comfortably, my Mind being entirely composed by resigning to the Will of God, and throwing my self wholly upon the Disposal of his Providence. This made my life better than sociable, for when I began to regret the want of Conversation, I would ask my self whether thus conversing mutually with my own Thoughts, and, as I hope I may say, with even God himself by Ejaculations, was not better than the utmost Enjoyment of humane Society in the World. [P. 107]

It is not that Crusoe considers himself a more amusing conversationalist than others might be, but that in "conversing mutually with [his] own Thoughts" Crusoe can trust and understand what is meant; conversing with God allows him the most truthful and consequent conversation. How Crusoe's isolation is superior emerges more fully in another passage:

> In the first Place, I was remov'd from all wickedness of the World here. I had neither the *Lust of the Flesh*, the *Lust of the Eye*, or the *Pride of Life*. I had nothing to covet; for I had all that I was now capable of enjoying: I was Lord of the whole Manor; or if I pleas'd, I might call my self King, or Emperor over the whole Country which I had possession of. There were no Rivals, I had no Competitor, none to dispute Sovereignty or Command with me. [P. 101]

The wonderful illusion here is that lust and pride are in society and not in the individual, that separated from the occasions for lust there would be no lust, that desire is purely external, and that there is an essential self that precedes society. Another perfection of isolation is that the island (or I-Land) experience admits no competitors, a delightful thought for the tradesman, whose constant worry was the rough competition of the marketplace. On the island, Crusoe is absolute master of his own life, a sovereign self in full possession of his land and production.

Certainly this utopian desire is an escape from the complexity of social dependence. But if we approach this contradiction from the view of narrative strategy, it appears in a different light. We see not a utopian dream separate from other matters but as part of a system of permissive allowances that affirms both sides of the contradiction. Crusoe can delight in the illusion of the sovereign self only on the basis of social supports he never relinquishes: first, because his life, even in the extreme setting of the island, is physically impossible without social products and techniques; second, because his pride of self requires the presence of the other (society) in order to be maintained; and third, because the very concepts by which he identifies himself are social and require the fantasy of being observed by others, i.e., thought of by the world to whom the writing is presented. Class ideology aims to suppress the conditions of its own existence—the full ensemble of social relations and the immense reservoir of culture—which cannot be its own creation, but the suppression is never even close to complete. As with all suppression, it is only partial and convenient. *Robinson Crusoe* confirms this interchange between the individual and society, even within the fantasy of a fully sovereign self.

At this point we can return to the question of the dramatic rejection of money to see how this knot is unwound in the text. Crusoe rejects money because it has no use value. As an independent producer who consumes directly what he produces, Crusoe has collapsed the long winding discourse of trade to its ultimate efficiency, production for use. The complex mediations of distribution and exchange, all that makes life so uncertain for the tradesman (but also the necessary condition for tradesmen), have been displaced. Money is the medium of exchange for this discourse of trade. But for all his showy rejection of money, Crusoe holds on to it in the same way that the notion of society, the other, is necessary for the fantasy of the sovereign self. He rejects money, but only in a way that keeps Crusoe's attention on it as the necessary condition for his satisfaction in being free from it. So, not surprisingly, we find constant references to money:

> Alas! There the nasty sorry useless Stuff lay; I had no manner of Business for it; and I often thought with my self, That I would have

given a Handful of it for a gross of Tobacco Pipes. . . . if I had had the drawer full of Diamonds, it had been the same Case; and they had been of no manner of Value to me, because of no Use. [P. 102]

These continuing attempts to exorcise the force of money, and by extension the idea of a complex circuit of trade, are hopeless because the fantasy of a private economy requires this constant reference to society.

As the narrative proceeds, money becomes the only true measure of Crusoe's life. In the same way, the fantasy of the sovereign self ultimately requires real human subjects to be anything other than a sorry illusion. Crusoe can play at being "Majesty the Prince and Lord of the whole Island" with his parrot, dog, and cats as subjects (pp. 116–17), but the appearance of that single footprint explodes his imaginative empire into mere whimsy and "wild ideas" (p. 121). The subjection of real men—first Friday and then the mutineers—is necessary to fix the sovereign self as anything other than fantasy. In the same way, money returns as the real measure of Crusoe's life. As the approach of others to his island becomes more obvious, Crusoe ceases his pious rejection of money. When a second ship is stranded on a nearby reef, Crusoe happily lugs home bags of coin, small bars and wedges of gold, without a moment of moralizing (pp. 150–51).

Later we discover that the accumulation of money is the *only* measure for Crusoe's life. When, after more than twenty years of isolation, Crusoe estimates what has been lost of his life, he remarks:

I might have been . . . one of the most considerable Planters in the *Brasils,* nay, I am perswaded, that by the Improvements I had made, in the little Time I liv'd there, and the Encrease I should probably had made, if I had stay'd, I might have been worth an hundred thousand Moydores. [P. 152]

And, indeed, when Crusoe returns, he finds his wealth has been accumulating with a life of its own, that his plantation has continued to spout money and, therefore, his life, apparently lost in his narrow sphere of private production, has returned to him—"the Value of the Plantation encreasing, amounted to 38,892 Cruisadoes, which made 3241 Moidores" (p. 220). There are no little Crusoes, but lots of Cruisadoes were spawned in his absence.

The permissiveness of narrative is at work here. It is senseless to reduce *Robinson Crusoe* to one pole of the contradiction and then charge Defoe with hypocrisy. The narrative constructs a field of possibilities and allows both the vision of independent economic production and, at the same time, the support and benefits of the vast complex of social relations. The tradesman must see his function as if it included production for use—and not only distribution and exchange for profit—if his ideology is to be able to claim totality. Exclude any of these moments in the economic circuit, and the tradesman appears dependent and socially implicated. His role in the world must be perceived as absolutely independent and also as fully immersed in the social complex, though only secondarily and as if in an afterthought. *Robinson Crusoe* puts on display for us the shape of this imaginary narrative.

One last observation, and perhaps the most important, on the difference between traditional concepts of ideology and the one developed in this discussion is necessary. In the traditional view, ideological justifications of class positions were seen merely as mystifications of social reality. The new view recognizes that ideological narratives do not have social reality, as such, as their object, but, instead, are shaped by hope and desire, by the most permissive version (given the constraints that cannot be excluded) of mastery over experience (closure) and also desire (open prospects). As such, the ideological narrative is both retrogressive (fixed in the justificatory tangle of a defensive class argument) but also progressive (aware of what is lacking to itself and desiring to provide for this lack). Thus, *Robinson Crusoe* demands an adventurous spirit, a direct experience of the world, against a morality that is static and feeble with smug privilege. When Crusoe turns against his father's tired wisdom, Defoe endorses a hearty confrontation with the world that is particular to that early bourgeois moment but is also the spirit of general historical progress.

The emphasis on productive labor in *Robinson Crusoe* is certainly another instance where the effort to legitimize a narrow class view must open out on values that, in practice, it cannot easily claim. Since the tradesman's world view must depict its role in the world as productive, the effort, discipline, and cunning of labor receives a rare and unexpected positive portrayal. Though labor is depicted in the limiting circumstances of private production, the novel does recognize the sundry tasks required to support life and the wit and application that belong to the laborer. *Robinson Crusoe* is an epic of labor and can still have the effect Rousseau ascribed to it of enlightening the naive or the overly sophisticated to the realities of the production of life in society.

Finally, when Defoe attempts to work his way through the difficulties of slavery, he discovers a strange desire to reach beyond the narrow cultural enclosure of Europe to other ways of being in the world. The moment comes when Crusoe is surprised by his servant Friday with a theological question that he, as a self-assured Christian catechist, cannot answer. While Friday is praised only for his servile virtues—his good humor, quick obedience, and full devotion to his master—in this instance Friday is accorded an independent intelligence and perhaps even an ironic perception of what Crusoe cannot see. At the very least, when Friday asks his devastating question, the confrontation between European and dark other is suddenly revealed not to be one-sided: "if God [i.e., your god] much strong, much might as the Devil, why God no kill the Devil so make him no more do Wicked?" (p. 170). Crusoe is not provided the wit of a professional catechist (though Defoe could certainly have provided him with arguments sufficient to win the debate—for that matter, could have had Friday not ask his question) and so is forced to retreat behind arguments he himself cannot affirm. For an instant the text puts its readers at the edge of a remarkable discovery: that the encounter with those other people opens out on new worlds and new gods and a gentle simplicity unknown to Crusoe's world of subtle calculation. And this is a necessary condition for ideological narrative because the desire for open windows to further adventures must provide openings in an otherwise closed picture through which can be seen the possibility for a differently constructed world that belongs to the future.

1. Raymond Williams, *Keywords: A Vocabulary of Culture and Society* (New York: Oxford University Press, 1976), pp. 126–30; also in *Marxism and Literature* (New York: Oxford University Press, 1977), pp. 55–71; see also George Lichtheim, "The Concept of Ideology," in *The Concept of Ideology and Other Essays* (New York: Random House, 1963), pp. 3–46.

2. Louis Althusser, "Marxism and Humanism," in *For Marx* (London: New Left Books, 1977), pp. 231–35.

3. See Pierre Macherey, *A Theory of Literary Production* (London: Routledge & Kegan Paul, 1978), pp. 75–101.

4. Ian Watt, "*Robinson Crusoe* as Myth," republished in revised form in *Robinson Crusoe,* ed. Michael Shinagel (New York: Norton, 1975), pp. 311–32. Original version in *Essays in Criticism: A Quarterly Journal of Literary Criticism* 1 (April 1951): 95–119.

5. Ibid., pp. 324, 326.

6. Ibid., p. 325.

7. Ibid., p. 321.

8. J. Paul Hunter, *The Reluctant Pilgrim: Defoe's Emblematic Method and Quest for Form in Robinson Crusoe* (Baltimore, Md.: Johns Hopkins University Press, 1966); George A. Starr, *Defoe and Spiritual Autobiography* (Princeton, N.J.: Princeton University Press, 1965).

9. John J. Richetti, *Defoe's Narratives: Situations and Structures* (Oxford: Clarendon Press, 1975), p. 7.

10. Ibid., pp. 14–15.

11. Ibid., p. 18.

12. Everett Zimmerman, *Defoe and the Novel* (Berkeley: University of California Press, 1975), p. 18.

13. Ibid., p. 44. Zimmerman's discussion is an important advance in one respect because he is willing to assert the remarkable disharmony of Defoe's novel. Since ideological thinking is always ready to claim unity and closure in a discourse, Zimmerman's approach provides a useful premise of deconstruction. However, he goes too far in seeing only chaotic disorder and misses the opportunity for discovering the intentional pattern of these disharmonies and the narrative maneuvers that aim to disguise them.

14. Peter Earle, *The World of Defoe* (New York: Atheneum, 1977), p. 113.

15. Ibid., pp. 118–19. Earle is summarizing an argument made in *A Brief State of the Inland or Home Trade of England* (1730) and in *The Complete English Tradesman* (1726–27).

16. Earle, *The World of Defoe,* p. 168; from Defoe, *Review* iii, p. 6.

17. Ibid., p. 193.

18. Ibid., p. 49; from Defoe, *Review* ix, pp. 109–10.

19. Ibid., p. 227; from Defoe, *Complete English Tradesman,* ii, pp. 190–91.

20. All references to *Robinson Crusoe* are to the Norton edition, ed. Michael Shinagel, and will be cited in the text.

21. Earle, *The World of Defoe,* p. 131; from Defoe, *Review* xi, p. 89.

22. Karl Marx, *The Grundrisse,* ed. and trans. David McLellan (New York: Harper Torchbooks, 1971), p. 17.

"To the Same Defect": Toward a Critique of the Ideology of the Aesthetic

James H. Kavanagh
Princeton University

T HIS essay will attempt a theoretical analysis of the ideology of the aesthetic. Like any other, my work proceeds from a problematic—a conceptual matrix that sets founding problems, opens specific paths of investigation, and therefore leads to specific kinds of solutions. The problematic of this essay derives from the work of Louis Althusser, Pierre Macherey, Etienne Balibar, Terry Eagleton, and Tony Bennett, and attempts to advance Marxism's understanding of various social and cultural activities as constitutive aspects of the class-divided socioeconomic formations that provide their condition of possibility.[1]

We note at the outset that our problematic does not pose the question, "What is the aesthetic?"—a form of interrogation that takes everything, namely the existence of the "aesthetic," for granted with its "What is . . . ?"[2] We investigate, rather, what kind of work one might do on the *ideology* of the aesthetic, insisting that the aesthetic can only be known, since it can only exist, in its effects, of which its accompanying ideology is one. We seek, then, not a descriptive analysis of the aesthetic as a given "real" object, but a theoretical analysis of the ideology that gives us, and is given to us by, the aesthetic. It is not a question of finding out what some "thing" called the aesthetic really is, but of producing a real concept of the process of production and consumption of those ensembles of effects we experience as aesthetic, a concept that will displace that experience with its explanation.

We must remark, too, on the special sense that the words *theory* and *ideology* have in our problematic. *Ideology*, for example, does not primarily signify a consciously articulated set of ideas that form the explicit basis of a political "world view," but a system of unconscious or preconscious image-concepts that form the implicit basis for a "lived" relation to the real. Ideology identifies a system of representations through which men and women *imagine* and *experience* as well as *think about* their relation to, and their place within, a given socioeconomic mode of production and its class structure. Indeed, strictly speaking, *ideology* signifies no "thing" at all, but a *type of relation*, "indispensable in any social formation," an "imaginary" relation of individuals to their real conditions of existence. This ideological relation constitutes the subject in a complex "reality" overdetermined by specular investments and by the necessity to enable practical activity.[3] Among other things, this relation does, indeed, give rise to "sets of ideas" and forms of representation, whose ideological character is given in their assumption of a complex preconstructed "reality" as a simple, unconstructed ground of their veracity. In literary studies, for example, such an ideological assumption can be seen in the appeal to the aesthetic or literary "text-itself."

A theory or science, on the other hand (and these two words have virtually the same meaning in this problematic), interrogates and breaks the seemingly natural, lived relation to a "reality" of world and subjectivity that an ideology constructs, revealing the active structuring presuppositions of which the ideology cannot be aware. The lived relation to a seemingly given real object is replaced with a theoretical relation to an explicitly constructed object of knowledge, a relation that enables the production of knowledges through internally constituted, virtually "subjectless," procedures. A theory or science of the aesthetic text would replace the aesthetic experience that such a text gives with the concept of what makes that experience possible in its specific form.

The difference between theory and ideology here is not the difference between *truth* and *error*. The relation of these categories is not one of pure negation or inversion. As Etienne Balibar emphasizes:

Ideology is a social instance, which is totally irreducible to the epistemological dimension of an error, an illusion or misrecognition. In given historical conditions ideology produces *"mis-recognition" effects* but it cannot be defined *as* misrecognition, that is, through its (negative) relation to knowledge. . . . The relation of science and ideology is therefore in all respects an unequal and heterogeneous relation in which the two terms cannot be spontaneously associated or "work" directly on each other without the intervention of a third term, practice.[4]

In this problematic, theories, like ideologies, only exist as specific *practices,* with theoretical and ideological practices forming (along with economic and political practices) two of the four major social practices that constitute a social formation. A given social formation is characterized by a specific, reciprocally interdetermining articulation of these four practices in which each finds its condition of possibility in the others. Each practice is, strictly speaking, a process of production, installed in institutions and apparatuses, using, according to its own appropriate procedures, raw materials (including products of the other practices), instruments of labor, and labor processes to produce specific effects indispensable to the functioning of the social whole. In complex social formations, each of these practices becomes further differentiated into a set of subpractices or activities whose specific effects have become important for a given social structure. In a class-divided society, ideological practices seek to effect a continual readequation of the subject's lived relation to a reality, giving it the force of a unified, coherent, eternal structure in which subjects find their rightful place and conflicts are resolved, disappear, or become transformed into supports of a given set of social relations.

We suggest that the aesthetic or the literary-aesthetic identifies a region of ideological practice. In modern critical discourses, the "aesthetic" is a sign under which proceed the production and consumption of specific ensembles of effects by ideological practices—practices that intervene in the subject's sense of a "lived relation to the real." The literary-aesthetic, then, is not only accompanied by, but indeed, can only exist as *part of,* an ideological apparatus whose task is precisely to break certain writing and reading practices off from others in order to constitute them as "aesthetic," "literary," "art," etc. Texts do not exist as aesthetic, except as encrusted in an "ideology of the aesthetic," or, more properly, only so exist as a recognized effect of that ideology, which is no external "encrustation," but the very condition of their existence—that which produces them and which they must reproduce. As Macherey and Balibar suggest: "Literary is the text recognized as such, and it is recognized as such precisely in the moment and in the measure that it activates interpretations, criticism, and 'readings'."[5]

It is important to recognize the sense in which such reflections eliminate the notion of the "text-itself" as a given object providing an unconstructed ground of veracity for criticism. The literary text, the aesthetic object, is not coterminous with the book we hold in our hands. The written book becomes a literary text not by virtue of some intrinsic quality that guarantees its aesthetic nature, but by virtue of its relation to an ideology of the literary-aesthetic that constructs it as such. The aesthetic is an effect of the ideology of the aesthetic, and the literary-aesthetic text is an effect of an operation that a literary-ideological practice performs on a written work. Of course, certain books come into the world preening themselves before this ideological practice, deliberately incorporating "intrinsic" qualities appropriate for the ideological operation of a literary-critical reading that they know awaits them. Indeed, in the modern world, *all* books are written in some relation to that possibility, even if it be negative. But the ideology of the aesthetic changes in concurrence with the demands of a given social formation on its ideological practices and no *book*, not even the antiliterary one, can guarantee its recognition or nonrecognition—that is, its construction as a "literary" or "aesthetic" *text*—by literary-ideological practices: "A text can very easily *stop* being literary, or *become* so under new conditions."[6]

If one were to ask *where* the aesthetic effect occurs, one would have to suggest that it occurs suspended, as it were, between eye and page, not in a phenomenological unity between subject and object but in an intersection of two practices in which subjectivity is constructed under complex determinations. Aesthetic effects, and meaning, occur in the space of contact between a set of writing gestures (*écriture*) and a reading gaze—a gaze that is itself formed by other texts and practices which intervene within the gaze to effect a complex, constructive relation that is experienced *as if* it were a simple "recognition."

Criticism has an ideological character precisely insofar as it tends unconsciously to assume the aesthetic as a quality inherent in certain texts previous to criticism's own operations, a quality that criticism either "finds" or does not, and a quality that, typically, exists in some inverse relationship to a work's "political" or "ideological" (same word, different problematic) qualities. The theory of criticism proposed here suggests, on the other hand, identifying how the aesthetic and the literary are founded in given social formations on the terrain of the ideological as particularly intense specifications of the ideological effect itself. Although the ideological is not synonymous with the political, and no intrinsic political significance is inscribed a priori in a given set of ideological effects, they are at any time always *attached to,* or affiliated with, specific political purposes.[7] Through its implication in the *ideological,* literature has the potential to adjust or disrupt social subjects' experience, imagination, and ideas of the social real in ways that can be politically significant.

The ideological, then, is not some unfortunate aspect of certain insufficiently aestheticized texts' ideational content, but a terrain of practice that serves as an indispensable condition of any text's existence *as* literary or aesthetic (or nonliterary, nonaesthetic). A text becomes literary when it is appropriately framed by a literary-ideological practice as a catalyst for constituting the reading subject in a lived relation to an assumed "reality" of the aesthetic. The more complex and hardworking the literary-ideological practice, the more the appropriate framing mechanisms appear as generated internally, "automatically," unconsciously, by text and reading subject.

What we call the aesthetic, then, is a double process of ideological production. Literary authorial labor applies always-already-ideologized linguistic and formal strategies to always-already-ideologized experiential, historical, and theoretical raw materials to produce certain "lived" effects. The textual effect, however, can only be realized in a second productive act—a labor of reading that takes up its own already-ideologized raw materials (including the text recognized as appropriately "written"[8] and applies its own already-ideologized transformative procedures for projecting meaning toward a given "lived" effect. Thus, the text can never be "itself"; it is always something other than itself.

Through its concept of ideology, the Althusserian concept of textual production understands the necessary relation of the literary to the historical and political as transiting the psycho-analytic and "imaginary." Indeed, part of the specificity of what we call aesthetic and literary procedures is that they achieve politically significant effect *indirectly,* by manipulating and re-constructing a "lived" experience in ways that always pass through an intense address to the unconscious (as well as through already constituted literary-aesthetic practices and dis-courses).

It is in these terms of the complex conditions of ideological production, I think, and not in terms of the eternal "charm" of Greek art (Marx) or of Dante's universal "genius" (Trotsky)—terms taken precisely from the ideology of the aesthetic—that Marxists can properly speak of the transhistorical dimensions of the putatively "aesthetic-effect."[9] In every human culture there have been intense modes of suggestive address that draw on raw materials and procedures which are effective beyond the historical and ideological conditions of their emergence—just as iron ore, steam energy, and labor power are usable in modern as well as ancient modes of production. But the point is precisely that the same or similar raw materials, procedures, and effects can be taken up in *different* modes of production, generating products that enter into radically different "systems of objects." If we tend to identify all such products as "aes-thetic," it is only because the specific ideology of the aesthetic that sets *our* "lived" relation to such gestures tends, like all ideologies, to present itself as universal and eternal, a language with which we read/rewrite every past.[10]

But Greek tragedy, the Roman epic, metaphysical poetry, and *The Faerie Queene,* are previous examples (or "ancestors") of "aesthetic" or "literary" objects only in the sense that chariots, wagons, and horses are previous examples (or "ancestors") of automobiles—which is to say, not at all. Partial congruences of material productive procedures, or even functions, do not an-nul the radical discontinuity in the objects produced and the systems in and for which they are produced. The automobile did not "descend" from the horse and buggy; it developed on another terrain and *displaced* it. Similarly, the novel did not "descend" from previously established forms we now call "liter-ature"; it developed on another terrain of productive ideological practice and displaced them.[11] In a characteristic ideological gesture, the ideology of the aesthetic here imparts an impression of unity, coherence, and continuity to a heterogeneous and conflicted field. The words *aesthetic* and *literary* can operate within a theoretical discourse as terms that denote a general function at an appropriate level of generality (something like "means of transportation" for chariots and cars) only if they are disinvested of all the special significance that is part of their very reason for existence right now—only if, that is, they come to signify something like "means of ideological production."

What, then, does a text have to do, or have to be seen as able to do, what means of ideological production in the form of textual effects enables a means of ideological production in the form of criticism to mark a work as literary, as participating in the "aesthetic"? As a way of emphasizing the specificity and historicity of the notion of the aesthetic in which we live, it is worth noting, first of all, what the aesthetic text does *not* have to do. It does not have to reproduce the harmony and order of God's cosmos or the heroic violence and discipline of the social order, or obey the fixed rules of a genre. So, despite our tendency to use it as an analogous notion, the modern notion of the "aesthetic" or the "literary" does *not* designate the same object as did "poetics," "poesie," "tragedy," or like concepts for previous thinkers: Plato, Aristotle, and Sidney were *not* writing about "literature" or "art," which did not yet exist. We are discussing a notion of the aesthetic and the literary specific to our historical epoch; its function is to readequate the subjectivity of agents of the bourgeois social formation and no others. We should not forget, as Raymond Williams reminds us, that "in its modern form, the concept of 'literature' did not emerge earlier than the eighteenth century and was not fully developed until the nineteenth century." Even if, as he points out, "the conditions for its emergence had been developing since the Renaissance," the word *literary* "did not acquire its specialized modern meaning until the eighteenth century."[12] And this "literature" emerges not just as a new post-Kantian *word* with which to rename something that has always existed; it emerges as an element of an entirely new problematic, the effect and condition of a *practice* of ideological production, itself emerging as a constituent element of modern industrial society and modern forms of class struggle.

Indeed, a key point of divergence between modern notions of the aesthetic and quasi-analogous classical or premodern notions is the former's overwhelmingly *favorable* evocation of individual expression, combined in various ways with an appeal to a corpus of works that preserve a kind of transhistorical cultural treasure, the product and heritage of an appropriately appreciative elite. This elite is now *not* explicitly defined in terms of social class but in terms of participation in a transhistorical dialogue of aesthetic expression. Thus, the modern ideology of the aesthetic has the very important function of effacing class contradiction—a function that does not indicate its "escape" from, but its specific form of implication in, a historically specific class society. Macherey and Balibar theorize this function by identifying modern literary language as a linguistic "[class-]compromise formation," an "intervention in the determination and reproduction of the contradictory linguistic practices of a common language."[13]

If there is a textual effect that marks both the classical and modern ideological practices we now identify as "aesthetic," it is what we can call the "reality-effect" or the "suggestion-effect"—the evocation of a persuasive, hypnagogic sense of reality in and through the mechanisms of the fictive—and this is precisely the effect that marks the aesthetic as intervening in the subject's sense of a "lived relation to the real," that is, in the ideological. This "reality-effect" is not congruent with what is traditionally called "realism,"[14] since it refers to the sense of the reality of, and/or within, the aesthetic object or "experience" itself rather than to any reference to an "outside" reality or experience:

> fiction and realism are not concepts *for* the production of literature, but, on the contrary, notions produced *by* literature. . . . *It is literary discourse which induces and projects in its midst the presence of the "real" in the manner of an hallucination.*[15]

In premodern thinking, this effect is identified as *transport, sublimity, probability,* terms that are *not* invested with the same values as our notion of the "aesthetic." But divergences between modern and premodern critical discourses reappear most markedly over the *value* (political, moral, "aesthetic") of this reality-effect: modern ideologies of the aesthetic tend to identify for us as natural and positive some of the very effects that classical thinkers (such as Plato) identified as unusual and/or dangerous.

The *modern* ideology of the literary-aesthetic identifies, under the sign of a special moral and cultural value, a certain ensemble of writing and reading activities through which the subject's readequation to the "reality" of a class-structured social formation is *driven* by the evocation of powerful and threatening libidinal cathexes, articulated in progressively more precocious linguistic and symbolic play. Thus, the categories of dreamwork analysis become cogent for analysis of both literature and its critical commentary (a point to which we shall return).

Premodern suspicions of this "reality" or "suggestion-effect" derive as well from the recognition that this play with one's sense of the real invokes a play with structures of unconscious, libidinal management—a play that can itself have potentially disruptive effects on the structure of a social order. Indeed, in their debates, classical thinkers produce, without recognizing it, a concept of the ideological that identifies one's sense of social reality and one's subject-ed place within it as thoroughly saturated with imaginary investments. Not for nothing did Aristotle and Plato frame their discourse accordingly:

> Does not the latter—I mean the rebellious principle—furnish a great variety of materials for imitation. . . . The imitative poet implants an evil constitution, for he indulges the irrational nature. . . . when any sorrow of our own happens to us, then you may observe that we pride ourselves on the opposite quality—we would fain be quiet and patient; this is the manly part, and the other which delighted us in the recitation is now deemed to be the part of a woman. . . . let us assure our sweet friend and the sister arts of imitation, that if she will only prove her title to exist in a well-ordered State we shall be delighted to receive her—we are very conscious of her charms.[16]

> In respect of Character there are four things to be aimed at. First and most important, it must be good. Now any speech or action that manifests moral purpose of any kind will be expressive of character: the character will be good if the purpose is good. This rule is relative to each class. Even a woman may be good, and also a slave; though the woman may be said to be an inferior being, and the slave quite worthless.[17]

Here, arguments about representations are clearly arguments about the desirability of evoking the repressed "feminine" and "rebellious" drives that threaten to disrupt a carefully fixed order of society and subjectivity—the point of disagreement is only over whether these drives can be managed once evoked. Perhaps Aristotle and Plato were able to identify the problem so explicitly because women and slaves could pose no real threat in their social order. In that sense, Plato's admonitions may be more farsighted. The project of setting "rules" for what we call "aesthetic" representation has been from the outset, then, allied to a project of social and libidinal management.

The modern production of the aesthetic seeks, as well, to manage severe contradictions, albeit on a different ideological terrain. The modern ideology of the aesthetic is at once much more reticent about class and social tensions and at the same time much bolder in assuming, displaying, and valorizing those textual effects which disrupt through suggestion the subject's sense of the real. Indeed, it is the problem of *managing* the accelerated dispersal of ideological power and effect that marks the production of the aesthetic as a conflicted ideological practice within a bourgeois social formation whose specific task is to promote an equal opportunity for individual initiative while reproducing its own class structure.

To be literary a modern text must be readable as reconciling the powerful demonstration of an arbitrary authorial agent's/text's ability to manipulate and transform the "real"—an ability that implies the specificity and historicity of the subject's lived relation to the real—with a powerful sense of that same authorial agent's/text's participation in an eternal, essential cultural nobility whose "reality" is unchangeable. Literary language must demonstrate to the subject a transformative relation to a contingent sense of the real, while fixing the subject in a reverential relation to the impermeable reality of the aesthetic. The latter, for the bourgeois subject who knows he or she has been properly trained to "appreciate" aesthetic reality, is also, of course, a self-reverential relation. For those who have not been so trained, it can only be a demeaning relation to their "betters" or their "oppressors" (depending on their training in passivity). Therefore, as Balibar and Macherey suggest, the "literary-effect" is also a domination-effect.[18] In our culture a text is "literature" insofar as it contributes to this class-determined ideology of the literary, and whether the text so contributes is not determined "in" the "text-itself" but in that massive, institutional, ideological apparatus of literary criticism and literary education whose purpose is to process and produce texts as "literature":

> the ideology of literature, itself a part of literature, [works] ceaselessly to *deny* this objective base—to represent literature supremely as "style," individual genius (conscious or natural), creativity, etc., as something outside (and above) the process of education, which can only disseminate and comment on literature in a drudging, hopeless effort that has no possibility of finally capturing it. At stake in this constitutive denegation is the objective status of literature as an historical ideological form—its specific relation to the class struggle. And the first and last commandment of literary ideology is "Thou shalt describe *all* forms of class struggle, *save* that which determines thine own self."[19]

It is a massive apparatus of paid functionaries that confidently produces the ideology of the aesthetic as a guarantor of the management of the effects of literary language. "Literature" is literary criticism's answer to the unasked question, "How do we render diverse discursive ideological practices into a coherent apparatus for the reproduction of a dominant ideology?" In some ways, such a Marxist analysis of the literary has, ironically, more respect than its traditional apologists for the real social function of literature:

> literary criticism is not an expensive luxury. To the contrary, as what has proved to be the most potent vehicle for the peddling of all sorts of ideological wares and mythologies, it is money well spent. The uses to which literary texts are put within the social process constitute the most privileged mode of reproduction and social relay of the bourgeois myths which disperse men and women into a frozen world of idealist and essentialist categories. Myths of creation, of genius, of man's essential nature, of the eternity and universality of the forms in which we express ourselves are all strongly supported in this way.[20]

In this sense, one might comment on the bourgeoisie's recurrent inability, in times of crisis, to support the propagation of a literary ideology through its institutions of higher and lower learning. This inability—"justified" through the transsignification of the metaphysical humanism that previously held literature sacred into its inverted double, the utilitarian pragmatism that now finds literature useless—can be understood as another sign of the bourgeois social order's inability to insure the conditions—this time the ideological conditions—for its own reproduction. Of course, even when functioning "perfectly," this apparatus is not so perfectly unified as it would like to believe; inscribed within it, in curious forms (like this essay), are the marks of the conflicted social field that is its support.

As presently installed in a functioning social apparatus, the problematic of the modern ideology of the aesthetic is nowhere more clearly outlined than at its birth, or, more properly speaking, the moment of its prehistory.[21] The question of textual management of politically significant ideological contradictions is nicely illustrated in that authorial subject which the bourgeois ideology of the aesthetic constitutes as its privileged progenitor and most sacred object—Shakespeare. *A Midsummer Night's Dream* provides an example of a profoundly threatening and threatened play, formed around questions of desire and obedience, representation and class power, haunted throughout by the threat of death. The play begins with Theseus, the duke, admonishing Hermia, who wants to choose her own husband, that she must yield to the command of her father, who "should be as a god" to her. "Question your desires," Theseus warns, or as duke he will enforce the father's choice as law, and Hermia will have "Either to die the death, or to abjure / Forever the society of men."[22] Of course, Hermia "consents not to give sovereignty" (1.1.82) to the Father under any Name (even that of the Law), and with her escape to the forest we see the consequences of a world in which all follow their own desires. Unlike Hippolyta, Theseus's intended (who learns properly to submit to the man who literally won her in conquest), Titania, the queen of the fairies, resists the "forgeries of jealousy" (2.1.81) and stubbornly refuses to yield to her husband/king over possession of the "little changeling boy" (2.1.120). In the ensuing battle for phallic and political power, Oberon's revenge gives us the sight of Titania chasing an ass, an all too apt image of a world in which, no longer ruled by the voice of the father/king, one is all the more capriciously ruled by the power of one's passions.

But into this familiar Shakespearean theatrical landscape of desire versus authority steps yet a third group of people from a social order rarely so active on the Shakespearean stage—a group of characters explicitly defined as artisanal workers (a carpenter, a joiner, a weaver, a bellows-mender, a tinker, and a tailor). These characters have a somewhat different problem

(or is it the same?): the problem of producing an *appropriate*—
that is, class-appropriate, and therefore politically acceptable—
dramatic representation. For them, for this Shakespearean
play, the issues of what we call ideological-aesthetic production
are inextricably linked with issues of social class and political
power:

> *Bottom:* Let me play the lion too. I will roar that I will do any
> man's heart good to hear me. I will roar, that I will make the Duke
> say, "Let him roar again, let him roar again."
>
> *Quince:* An you should do it too terribly, you would fright the
> Duchess and the ladies, that they would shriek; and that were
> enough to hang us all.
>
> *All:* That would hang us, every mother's son.
>
> *Bottom:* I grant you, friends, if you should fright the ladies out of
> their wits, they would have no more discretion but to hang us: but I
> will aggravate my voice so that I will roar you as gently as any
> sucking dove; I will roar you an 'twere any nightingale.
>
> [1.2.71–85]

We might take this dialogue as a Shakespearean treatise on
aesthetics.[23] It is a discourse that dispels its own retrospective
mystification by the ideology of the aesthetic, and displays the
political problematic of the production of aesthetic effects at
the dawn of the bourgeois era.[24] These workers pose the issues
quite clearly in their discussion: for *us* to assert an effective
ability to manipulate *their* sense of "reality," for *us* to produce a
reality-effect over *them,* would be an unacceptable usurpation
of ideological power, possibly punishable by death; we must
temper our dramatic practice, restrain its effect, and inscribe in
it the marks of our own submission. That the noble lords and
ladies laugh at these players' fear only confirms the political
and ideological conditions which make it possible. The anxious
emergence of what we call bourgeois realism—an increasingly
sophisticated manipulation of the reality-effect—is partly
defined by this sense of the unforeseeable consequences of *us*
making *them* scream or of getting the noble ladies overexcited.

The artisans attempt to solve their problem by inventing a
first version of an estrangement-effect:

> *Bottom:* Masters, you ought to consider with yourselves. To bring
> in—God shield us—a lion among ladies, is a most dreadful thing.

For there is not a more fearful wild fowl than your lion living; and
we ought to look to't.

Snout: Therefore another prologue must tell he is not a lion.

Bottom: Nay, you must name his name, and half his face must be
seen through the lion's neck, and he himself must speak through,
saying thus, or to the same defect—"Ladies"—or, "Fair Ladies—I
would wish you"—or, "I would request you"—or, "I would entreat
you—not to fear, not to tremble: my life for yours. If you think I
come hither as a lion, it were pity of my life. No I am no such thing.
I am a man as other men are." And there indeed let him name his
name, and tell them plainly, he is Snug the joiner.

[3.1.28–46]

This actually inverts the Brechtian alienation aesthetic, displaying the conditions of aesthetic production—of aesthetic effect and "defect"[25]—not in order to enable a working-class audience intelligently to assert its political power but to enable this
workers' troupe to *escape* the political power of a ruling class.
And, of course, it is we, and not Shakespeare, who register
these players as precursors of "working-class" figures in our
sense of the word; for him, the image of artisanal workers
comically annuls any sense of real threat, precisely because they
are so marginal and incapable of exerting effective power in his
social formation—as were women and slaves for Aristotle and
Plato.

Indeed, these figures invoke not a nonexistent contem-
poraneous "working class" but a real emergent bourgeois aesthetic practice, forming within unprecedented conditions of
economic independence from aristocratic patronage while still
held within the ideological and political domination of aristocratic class relations. As Alvin Kernan notes, "although the facts
are well known, it seems still not to be well understood that the
English Renaissance dramatists, Shakespeare included, were
the first writers to work in the marketplace situation which has
since become the characteristic social and economic condition
of the literary artist."[26] In such a context, we can see how, as
Macherey and Balibar suggest, the problematic of bourgeois
aesthetic practice founds itself on "linguistic [class-]compromise
formations," embodying "*an unequal and contradictory relation* to
the *same ideology*—the dominant one," a contradiction that
"would not exist if the dominant ideology did not have con-

stantly to struggle for its priority."[27] Thus, Shakespearean language, the literary sign par excellence—indeed, the very sign *of*
the literary—forges from conflicted ideological semes an

> imaginary solution of implacable contradictions . . . in the sense of
> providing a *"mise en scène,"* a *"presentation as solution"* of the very
> terms of an insurmountable contradiction, by means of complex
> displacements and substitutions. For there to be literature, the very
> terms of the contradiction . . . must be enunciated at the outset in a
> special language . . . realizing *in advance* the fiction of their forth-
> coming conciliation—a language of "compromise" which presents
> the conciliation as "natural," and ultimately as necessary and inevi-
> table.[28]

Shakespeare, the play*wright* is, in effect, toying with his aristocratic audience. Drawing ideological raw materials from both
insurgent bourgeois-individualist and entrenched feudal-
absolutist discourses, and explicitly acknowledging the subversive implications of what he is doing at the moment, he then
continues to do it—in the form of a *submission* to that audience,
trivializing his threat within a *comedy* that prepares a resolution
for *A Midsummer Night's Dream* which magically reconciles
rebellious "feminine" desire to a rigid social hierarchy of aristocratic and patriarchal privilege.

In later contexts, when the bourgeoisie holds economic,
political, *and* ideological power, the problematic of aesthetic
practice will set the task of effectively representing the contradictions of bourgeois society to a mass audience without arous-
ing the suppressed political power of the dominated classes.
This task will require that increasingly complex class differentiation of audiences which the category "literature" (with its
obverse, "nonliterature") helps to promote. Shakespeare's for-
tunate, "accidental" choice of "pre-working-class" characters allows us to read his scenes, presented in a period of changing
conditions of aesthetic production, as registering on many different levels for us in a period of transformation in the modes
and theory of literary criticism.

In subsuming such work within a mythical notion of "Shakespeare" as a founding father of a transhistorical elite of
"geniuses" in sensitive communication with the eternal forms of
"beauty" and/or the "aesthetic," the modern ideology of the

aesthetic effaces the radically conflicted character of the work
on heterogeneous ideological raw materials that produces what
we call "literary" language. The modern ideology of the "literary-aesthetic" repeats rather than explains the illusion of truth,
beauty, perfect comedy, and coherence that is the effect of an
authorial subject's specific, complex type of ideological labor. If
Shakespeare's work is a kind of ideological production, the
critic's work must be a theoretical production—a kind of work
that explains both the different, radically discontinuous, historical modes of ideological production that address, fascinate,
worry, and fix social subjects in ways appropriate to the reproduction of a given social order, *and* the various ways in which
criticisms "resume" the ideological work of the texts whose
address they echo.

In this regard, Macherey and Balibar make a telling analogy
between an ideological criticism's account of its text and an
analysand's account of his or her dream. Neither discourse *explains;* both repeat what has to be explained, producing alter-
nate versions of the manifest content. One reads the dream/
text precisely by reading the *account* of the dream/text as its
ideology.

> That is why it is possible (and necessary) when analyzing the
> literary effect as produced qua text and by means of the text to treat
> as equivalents the "reader" and the "author." Also equivalent are
> the "intentions" of the author . . . and the interpretations, criticisms,
> and commentaries evoked from its more or less sophisticated
> readers.
> It is not important to know whether the interpretation "really"
> identifies the author's intention (since the latter is not the cause of
> literary effects but is one of the effects). Interpretations and com-
> mentaries reveal the literary aesthetic effect precisely in full view.
> Freud was the first to follow this procedure in his account of the
> dream-work and, more generally, in his method of analyzing the
> compromise formations of the unconscious; he defined what must
> be understood by the "text" of the dream. He gave no importance
> to restoring the manifest content of the dream—to a careful
> isolated reconstruction of the "real" dream. Or at least he accedes to
> it only through the intermediary of an "account of the dream"
> which is *already* a transposition through which (via condensation,
> displacement and dream symbolism) the repressed material con-
> tinues to work itself out. He also considered as the text of the
> dream—simultaneously the object for analysis and explanation,
> and, through its very contradictions, the means of its own explana-
> tion—not just the initial manifest text, the account of the dreamer,
> but also *all* the "free" associations (i.e., the forced associations im-

posed by the psychic conflicts of the unconscious), the "latent thoughts" for which the dream-account (or symptom) can serve as a pretext and which it arouses.

In the same way, critical discourse—the discourse of literary ideology, an endless commentary of the "beauty" and "truth" of literary texts—is a train of "free" associations (in actuality, forced and predetermined) which develops and realizes the ideological effects of a literary text. In a materialist account of the text, such a discourse must be taken not as located *above* the text, as the beginnings of its explication, but as *at the same* level as the text, or, more precisely, at the same level as the "surface" narrative. . . . Such a criticism constitutes the tendential prolongation of this facade. Regardless of any question of the *individuality* of the "writer," the "reader" or the "critic," it is the same ideological conflicts, resulting in the last instance from the same historical contradictions, or from their transformations, that produce the form of the text and its commentaries.[29]

We can take, for example, a gloss on Shakespeare by a prominent critic, a gloss that gives us elements for explaining a certain mode of aesthetic production while obstinately misrecognizing them. In *A Natural Perspective*, Northrop Frye remarks that "Shakespeare had no opinions, no values, no philosophy, no principles of anything except dramatic structure."[30]

One could more accurately say that the last thing Shakespeare might have had any opinions about was "dramatic structure" in the sense that Northrop Frye uses the notion, invested as it now is with two hundred years of a discourse on the "literary" and the "aesthetic" whose most basic terms could not be uttered until two hundred years after Shakespeare wrote-acted-staged-made money—and thought about all those things. "Dramatic structure" in Frye's sentence is unutterable and unreadable, and the concept it evokes unimaginable, by any Shakespeare but Frye's own, and *Frye himself tells us this. In preparation* for making the above statement, he insists: "His [Shakespeare's] chief motive in writing, apparently, was to make money." This motive Frye goes on to treat as having *no effect at all*, other than to provide transparent access to the literary, as he continues the sentence: "which is the best motive for writing yet discovered, as it creates exactly the right blend of detachment and concern."[31]

It is in such discourses that historically determinate aesthetic practices are recuperated for essentialist categories. It is not as if one reads Frye in order to understand Shakespeare (indeed, it may well be the other way around); one must read Frye *as* one reads Shakespeare. By no means is what is said *false;* it is a discourse, rather, in which truths are presented but not recognized, presented in a context that renders them more effective for the production of ideology than of knowledge.[32]

In the face of such discourses, the task of a historical materialist theory of literary ideology is threefold: (1) to explain and analyze the determination, the socioideological conditions of possibility of ideologies of the literary, historically, and in the present; (2) to intervene *in* the ideology of the literary toward the revalorization of canonical and insurgent writing practices; (3) to *replace* the notion of the literary and/or the aesthetic as founding, preceding, and inhering in certain texts conceived as objects in themselves, with the concept of text as the operator of a relation between historically determinate, ideologically and theoretically preconstructed, reading and writing practices, one of whose possible effects is the sense of the "literary," the sense of the "aesthetic"; that is, to recognize

> the notion of "the work" (and its correlative "the author") only to identify both as necessary illusions inscribed in *the ideology of literature that accompanies* all literary production. The text is produced under conditions which represent it as a finished work, displaying an essential order, expressing either a subjective theme or the spirit of the age, according to whether the reading is a naive or sophisticated one. Yet, in itself, the text is none of these; on the contrary, it is materially incomplete, disparate and incoherent, since it is the conflicted, contradictory effect of superimposing real processes which cannot be abolished in it except in an imaginary way.[33]

We are in a curious period in the historical life span of the ideology of the aesthetic—close not to its birth but to its death. Yet this is also the time of its ripeness, its absolute fruition. The means of production of transformative ideological effects have taken on a social character, a differentiation, and a sophistication that in practice render impotent any concept of the "aesthetic" in the sense that the word has been used during the past two hundred years. Benjamin's point needs only slight reformulation: there can be no work of "art" in the age of electronic reproduction. And yet the ideological institutions of our society have successfully fixed in almost every social subject a sense of awe in the face of the fetishized representations of a transhistorical genius—an elite in which they either know they will never participate or secretly believe that they already do. Which category one falls into depends, of course, on which class-articulated ideological institution has prepared one for which function in society.

The ideology of the aesthetic is truly, as Coleridge knew only it could be, the social analogue of religion in our secular age, exuding a pervasive and tenacious idealist notion of "culture" as the *soul* of society. The aesthetic is a realm in which we project a totalizing power that gives a sense of coherence in a world falling apart before our eyes, a realm in which we alienate our own social power to make the world whole into mythical figures who either strike us dumb and sullen or carry on with us a secret, private conversation—the ideal mirror-inversion of the world of fetishized commodities. The aesthetic is a means of attributing magical qualities to processes of ideological transformation whose real function and effect we desperately need to know and to use intelligently. There is something important and *effective* at stake here, a skill that has been developed and will not go away—and which, as we are coming to understand, demonstrates its contradictory possibilities at every social level, from the Metropolitan to the soap opera:

> the literary effect is not just produced by a determinate process but actively inserts itself within the process of *reproduction* of other ideological effects. . . . as ideological effect [it] is not just in the domain of "feeling," "taste," "judgement," and hence of aesthetic and literary "ideas"; it compels a set of practical activities: the active rituals of literary consumption and "cultural" practice.[34]

Our explanation of this effect must be disinvested of magical connotation, without being drained of its specificity.[35] We should remember that, like religion in a previous age, the aesthetic is an indispensable region of ideological practice that can only solve the problem of seeming to solve problems it cannot. Like religion in a previous age, it is an idiom in which contradictions are engaged and effaced, contradictions whose resolution will finally be determined on another terrain of activity, which our theoretical practice must always keep in sight—the terrain of the political.

1. Particularly relevant to the topic of this essay are Terry Eagleton's chapter "Marxism and Aesthetic Value" in *Criticism and Ideology* (London: New Left Books, 1976); Tony Bennett, *Formalism and Marxism* (London: Methuen, 1979); Pierre Macherey, "The Problem of Reflection," *Sub-stance*, no. 15 (1976), pp. 6–20; Macherey and Etienne Balibar, "Literature as an Ideological Form: Some Marxist Hypotheses," *Praxis* 5 (1980): 43–58. See also Macherey's *A Theory of Literary Production* (London: Routledge, 1977) and James H. Kavanagh, "Marks of Weakness: Ideology, Science, and Textual Criticism," *Praxis* 5 (1980): 23–38. *Praxis* 5 contains helpful articles, reviews, and bibliographical essays on Althusserian cultural studies.

2. As Macherey notes: "To ask this question ["What is literature?"], even implicitly, is to assume that literature is something—i.e., a totality unified by a coherent system of principles which assures its conformity to an essence given once and for all, and hence unchangeable." "The Problem of Reflection," p. 17. Throughout this essay I shall treat the "literary" as a subcategory of the "aesthetic."

3. See Althusser's essays "Humanism and Marxism," in *For Marx*, trans. Ben Brewster (New York: Vintage Books, 1970), and "Ideology and Ideological State Apparatuses," in *Lenin and Philosophy*, trans. Ben Brewster (New York: Monthly Review Press, 1971).

4. Etienne Balibar, "From Bachelard to Althusser: The Concept of Epistemological Break'," *Economy and Society* 7, no. 3 (August 1978): 224.

5. Macherey and Balibar, "Literature as an Ideological Form," p. 56.

6. Ibid.

7. Edward Said argues for the use of Gramsci's notion of "affiliation," in "Reflections on Recent American 'Left' Literary Criticism," *Boundary 2* 7, no. 1 (Fall 1979):11–30.

8. See Macherey and Balibar, "Literature as an Ideological Form," p. 55 and chaps. 2 and 3 of Eagleton's *Criticism and Ideology*.

9. We cite these passing formulations of Marx and Trotsky for our own purposes without meaning to dismiss all of their reflections on art and culture. Our theory does not characterize a discourse as ideological according to the fact *that* it incorporates or represents ideological "semes"—*no* discourse can be "ideology-free"!—but according to *how* the discursive practice systematically puts all its raw materials *into production*. We offer the following formulation, which will have to await full justification in another essay: the *necessary* presence of specific ideological elements does not suffice to distinguish an ideological from a scientific discursive practice, while the *necessity of* such elements being present does not annul the possibility of so distinguishing among discursive practices. See Eagleton's positive interpretation of Marx's comments on Greek art, in *Marxism and Literary Criticism* (Berkeley: University of California Press, 1976), pp. 9–13.

10. See Macherey, "The Problem of Reflection," p. 10:

"From where comes the eternal charm of Greek art?" There is no good answer to this question because there is no eternal charm to Greek art. The *Iliad*, a piece of universal literature . . . is not at all the one which the material life of the Greeks produced; the latter was not a "book," nor even a "myth" in the sense that we understand it and which we would like to apply in retrospect. Homer's *Iliad*, that is to say the "work" of an "author," exists only for us, with respect to the new material conditions in which it has been reinscribed and reinvested with a new meaning: as strange as this may seem, the *Iliad* did not exist for the Greeks, and thus the problem of conserving it does not present itself. Let us go further: everything happens as if we had composed or at least rewritten it ourselves. Works of art are processes, not things, because they are never produced once and for all but are always subject to being "reproduced"; they do not find even an identity or a content except in this incessant transformation. There is no eternal art, nor are there unchanging works of art.

11. These remarks are not meant to suggest that there is *no* relation between, or historical evolution of, genres. Clearly the development of any new genre presumes productive and consumptional signifying skills developed by previous genres—indeed, even a kind of exhaustive saturation of signifying practice with such skills. But the relation of new genres to old is more that of "cousins" than of "descendants," a relation that can be aptly reassembled and retotalized only against the constitutive ground of a social field—with analytic tools that must function at least *like* a theory of ideology.

12. Raymond Williams, *Marxism and Literature* (New York: Oxford University Press, 1977), pp. 46–47.

13. Macherey and Balibar, "Literature as an Ideological Form," p. 48. We will enlarge on this below. Macherey and Balibar draw heavily on the work of Renée Balibar, Geneviève Merlin, and Gilles Tret, in *Les Français fictifs: Le rapport des styles littéraires au français national* (Paris: Hachette, 1974), and *Le Français national: Politique et pratique de la langue nationale sous la Révolution* (Paris: Hachette, 1974).

14. Nor is it exactly congruent with Barthes's "*effet du réel.*"

15. Macherey and Balibar, "Literature as an Ideological Form," p. 54.

16. Plato, *Republic* 10, included in Walter Jackson Bate, *Criticism: The Major Texts* (New York: Harcourt, 1970), pp. 47–48.

17. Aristotle, *Poetics* 15, in Bate, p. 28. Those who have promoted an aesthetics under the sign of "Marxism" are not exempt from such an analysis. In his *Studies in European Realism,* Georg Lukács relates an incident in which Gorki struck a widow with a shovel during an argument, and praises Gorki for "never allow[ing] himself to be dragged down, even an instant, into her atmosphere of beastliness and filth. . . . For all the coarseness of the whole anecdote, it yet expresses Gorki's manliness, inner purity and delicacy no less distinctly than all his other manifestations and all his writings." Maynard Solomon emphasizes this anecdote in *Marxism and Art: Essays Classic and Contemporary* (Detroit, Mich.: Wayne State University Press, 1979), p. 392.

18. Macherey and Balibar, "Literature as an Ideological Form," p. 15.

19. Ibid., p. 48.

20. Tony Bennett, *Formalism and Marxism,* p. 170.

21. See comment below on the peculiarly "modern" conditions of Elizabethan dramatic production.

22. From *The Complete Signet Classic Shakespeare* (New York: Harcourt, 1972), 1.1.65–66.

23. We can do so only by removing it from its context within the play as a system of ideological production, and putting it into play within our own process of theoretical production.

24. We refer here, again, to the specific and precise sense, noted below, in which Shakespearean theater can be seen as a precursor of bourgeois modes of ideological-aesthetic production.

25. "Defect" is the original word of the first quartó of 1600, left unchanged in the second quarto and First Folio. See *The Signet Shakespeare,* p. 529.

26. Alvin Kernan, "Shakespeare's Stage Audiences: The Playwright's Reflections

and Control of Audience Response," unpublished manuscript. See also, Christopher Hill, *Reformation to Industrial Revolution, 1530–1780,* volume 2 of *The Pelican Economic History of Britain* (Harmondsworth: Penguin, 1969), pp. 87–90.

27. Macherey and Balibar, "Literature as an Ideological Form," p. 48.

28. Ibid., p. 50.

29. Ibid., p. 57.

30. Northrop Frye, *A Natural Perspective* (New York: Harcourt, 1965), p. 39. The comments I extract from Frye's work are no more meant to indicate its general value than were the comments I extracted from Marx, Trotsky, and Lukács meant to indicate their works' general value.

31. Ibid., p. 38.

32. When Frye says, for example, that "it is consistent with Shakespeare's perfect objectivity that he should show no signs of wanting to improve his audience's tastes, or to address the more instructed members of it with a particular intimacy" (p. 38), he describes a real and important characteristic of Shakespearean dramatic practice. This is *not,* however, a characteristic that marks Shakespeare as a "perfectly objective," "great poet" (p. 39), but one that marks him as not at all implicated in the "literature" which is reproduced by such terms precisely as a practice that addresses its more sophisticated audience "with a particular intimacy."

33. Macherey and Balibar, "Literature as an Ideological Form," p. 50.

34. Ibid., p. 56.

35. "From a materialist point of view, one would analyze *literary effects* (more precisely, aesthetic literary effects) as effects irreducible to ideology 'in general,' precisely because they are particular ideological effects *among others* (religious, juridical, political) on which they *depend,* and from which they *differ.*" Ibid., p. 55.

Panzani Pasta Advertisement.

Pasta, Barthes, and Baudrillard

Ronald L. Bogue
University of Georgia

"PÂTES–SAUCE–PARMESAN À L'ITALIENNE DE LUXE" reads the caption of a Panzani advertisement that Roland Barthes analyzes in his essay "Rhetoric of the Image," a 1964 study of the semiotics of the photograph.[1] But the linguistic communication interests Barthes less than the visual message that the caption supplements, a message that Barthes sees as dual: a connotative, symbolic message and a denotative, non-symbolic message. The symbolic message is multifaceted. The photograph in question depicts a half-opened, netlike shopping bag whose contents appear to be spilling forth onto a table. The prominent items in the bag, arranged in a diagonal descending from left to right, are two packages of Pâtes Panzani (in the bag), a can of Salsa Panzani (on the handle of the bag, half in, half out), and a package of Parmesan Panzani (out of the bag, leaning on a tomato and a mushroom cap). Secondary contents of the bag are onions, tomatoes, and green peppers (situated beneath the Panzani products). Barthes distinguishes four signs in this image: (1) a return from the market, indicated by the half-open bag, grounded in a knowledge of cultural habits of shopping; (2) *italianité,* the signifiers being the food items and the colors red, yellow, and green, reinforced by the linguistic message, both indirectly (the name Panzani) and directly ("à l'italienne"); (3) "the idea of a total culinary service" (p. 34), in that Panzani supplies all the ingredients for a spaghetti dinner and that the contents of the salsa can are the equivalent of the natural products surrounding it; (4) an aesthetic composition similar to a still-life painting.

These coded connotations do not exhaust for Barthes the

messages communicated by the photograph. If the images in the photograph are signifiers, their signifieds also are the real objects that were photographed. These signifiers do not transform the signifieds as do words, but analogically represent them in a mechanical, "objective" manner. What defines this message is "precisely that the relation between signified and signifier is quasi-tautological; . . . in other words, the sign of this message is not drawn from an institutional stock, is not coded, and we are brought up against the paradox . . . of a *message without a code*" (p. 36). This is the photograph's denotative message, a message Barthes finds suspect because it functions as a natural support for an ideological communication: "the absence of code disintellectualizes the message because it seems to found in nature the signs of culture" (pp. 45–46).

We can recognize here a concern of Barthes's dating back at least to the essay "Myth Today" in *Mythologies* (1957), where the denotation/connotation distinction is used to expose bourgeois myths that pose as empirical facts. (Barthes has stated often that the essence of bourgeois ideology is to deny that it is an ideology—that is, to pretend to the status of transparency.) Barthes concludes in "Myth Today" that "what allows the reader to consume myth innocently is that he does not see it as a semiological system but as an inductive one. Where there is only an equivalence, he sees a kind of causal process: the signifier and the signified have, in his eyes, a natural relationship."[2]

The photograph, then, is particularly insidious, for it presents a relationship of equivalence (its connotative message) in a natural relationship (its denotative message). (In "Myth Today," the most powerful example of ideology Barthes cites is a *photograph* of a black soldier in a French uniform.) The photograph compounds deception since the syntagmatic and paradigmatic (or in Barthes's terminology, systemic) aspects of this code—those inextricable functions of combination and selection basic to any semiological system, as Barthes states in *Elements of Semiology*—are apportioned to the denotative and connotative messages respectively. The connotative symbols in the Panzani advertisement are discontinuous and isolated, selected from various cultural codes that are held together in a syntagmatic relationship by the real space which the photograph denotatively represents. Hence Barthes's summation in "Rhetoric of the Image": "We can now understand that *it is precisely the syntagm of the denoted message which 'naturalizes' the system of the connoted message.* Or again: connotation is only system, can only be defined in paradigmatic terms; iconic denotation is only syntagm, associates elements without any system: the discontinuous connotators are connected, actualized, 'spoken' through the syntagms of the denotation, the discontinuous world of symbols plunges into the story of the denoted scene as though into a lustral bath of innocence" (p. 51).

What is to be made of this analysis? One must be immediately suspicious of the pairing of denotation and syntagm and of connotation and paradigm (or system). Are the symbols in the Panzani advertisement "discontinuous"? Is it true that "although the *Panzani* poster is full of 'symbols,' there nonetheless remains in the photograph, insofar as the literal message is sufficient, a kind of natural *being-there* of objects" (p. 45)? Is there no order to the presentation of the connotative signs since the photograph's order is "not linear" (p. 34)? I believe that the connotative messages Barthes discerns are organized in a hierarchical fashion, that one level of connotation dictates the syntagmatic relations of the objects in the photograph, and that the coded composition of the scene undermines the denotative "presence" of the signified objects. The support for the values that the advertisement connotes is not the real collection of objects but a narrative, inferred from this pregnant moment of the story, which combines two of the signs Barthes isolates: the trip to market and a total culinary service. The narrative is as follows: someone (Panzani hopes the reader of the advertisement will put himself in this role) goes to the store, buys ingredients for a spaghetti dinner, comes home, and prepares and consumes (with delight) such a repast. The photograph formally encodes the narrative: the prominent elements of the story (basket and Panzani products) are arranged in a well-lit diagonal, the basket *containing* the Panzani products since it represents the link between market and home, yet allowing some of the products to overflow, since it is the conduit by way of which goods gush into the kitchen, its diagonal proceeding from background to foreground, a suggestion of temporal movement from market past to kitchen present. The Panzani products are syntagms of the spaghetti recipe, which is cited as a preparation process by the inclusion of the products in the market narrative represented by the basket.

All elements of the photograph can be subsumed within this

narrative, whose unified action might be summarized as "to cook spaghetti dinner," if the fresh vegetables are to be combined with the canned salsa (this would be the "realistic" reading of the plot), but clearly the vegetables are part of a secondary narrative (as Barthes implies): the history of the manufacture of the salsa, which insures that the can is merely a translation of wholesome, natural foods into a more convenient form. That this is an ancillary narrative is indicated by the shadows which engulf most of the vegetables and by their literally subordinate position *underneath* the Panzani products.

Already a priority is implicit in the photographic message: first the market narrative, then the history of the manufacture of salsa. These narratives serve as the ground for other connotations. *Italianité* presents itself as mere fact (we of course recognize this as *institutional* fact, not *brute* fact): Italians eat spaghetti, Panzani is an Italian name and happens to be the name of an Italian pasta company, and the fresh vegetables displayed are ingredients in spaghetti salsa. It is the market narrative that naturalizes this connotation. The connotation is identifiable because we possess a reading competence that allows us to classify the photograph as an advertisement; any number of connotations may be generated by the objects in the image, but experience with the conventions of advertising allows us to expect self-congratulatory claims of authenticity, and *italianité* is one such claim. (The incorporation of the colors red, yellow, and green within *italianité* is a secondary benefit of the salsa-manufacture narrative, an instance of ideological overdetermination.)

The composition of the advertisement as a still life is also a secondary message, in that the values it communicates are not to be understood but felt as spontaneous effusions of the primary narrative. The still life is a metasign, a sign of the collection of signs in the photograph considered as a unity. The still life is of a particular sort—the cornucopia—and it conveys the gestural content of the advertisement: both the loving caress and monumentalization of the material world found in most still lifes, and the gift of material plenty offered by the advertisers in this moment, not of expenditure, but of immediate gratification.

In this sense the aesthetic reference effectively promotes the product, but in another sense it undermines the sales effort. Barthes claims that the advertisement contains no reference to itself as advertisement, yet, to the extent that the still life today has been replaced by the advertisement photograph (where else does one see still lifes outside the collections of old masterpieces in museums?), the utilization of the convention of the advertisement–as–still life declares the status of the advertisement as an effort at manipulation. The still-life convention of selecting only a few, symbolic objects for a composition also subverts the ends of the advertisement: the decontextualized, schematized elements of the Panzani poster hardly testify to the objects' *having-been-there*, which Barthes identifies as the primary, evidential, denotative message of the photograph ("Rhetoric of the Image," pp. 44–45); this bag of goods suspended in an undifferentiated space seems instead *never to have been anywhere*. The material reality of the signifieds is subsumed within the ideality of the conventional world of advertising.

The photograph's syntagmatic organization, then, can be explained without reference to the denotative message that Barthes isolates, and the levels of connotation can be organized into a hierarchy of priority—a priority that the linguistic message reinforces: first "Pâtes–sauce–parmesan" (the narrative of the dish's preparation), then "à l'italienne" (*italianité*, authenticity), then "de luxe" (quality, luxury, plenty). Advertising, far from depending on a message without code, in fact de-realizes the natural and designates it as cultural.

Yet perhaps the advertisement photograph is an exceptional genre, one so conventionalized that it counteracts the photograph's "natural" denotative message. Can we state, then, that *most* photographs have a denotative, natural content? Such a claim cannot be made without some qualification, which Barthes realizes. In his 1961 essay "The Photographic Message" (*Image/Music/Text*, pp. 15–31), Barthes isolates six techniques a photographer can wield to control his images: (1) trick effects; (2) arranging the pose of his subject; (3) including objects burdened with stereotypical associations in his composition; (4) embellishing the image through the manipulation of lighting, exposure, and printing; (5) aestheticizing the image by quoting from painting or sculpture; and (6) arranging photographs in groups. To the extent that the photographer uses these techniques the image takes on a cultural shape. But at an even more basic, perceptual level the photograph may be said to be laden with connotation: "if, as is suggested by certain hypotheses of Bruner and Piaget, there is not perception with-

out immediate categorization, then the photograph is ver-
balized in the very moment it is perceived," states Barthes.
"From this point of view, the image—grasped immediately by
an inner metalanguage, language itself—in actual fact has no
denoted state, is immersed for its very social existence in at least
an initial layer of connotation, that of the categories of language ("The Photographic Message," pp. 28–29). Is there then
no denotative message in a photograph? Barthes says that such
a message exists, for though denotation never appears without
connotation, denotation may be isolated as "what is left in the
image when the signs of connotation are mentally deleted"
("Rhetoric of the Image," p. 42). The denotative message is
"the letter of the image" that "corresponds in short to the first
degree of intelligibility . . . but this intelligibility remains virtual
by reason of its very poverty, for everyone from a real society
always disposes of a knowledge superior to the merely an-
thropological and perceives more than just the letter" (p. 42).
Hence the denoted image is "a kind of Edenic state of the
image" (p. 42). Barthes apparently maintains this category of
the virtual "letter of the image" because he sees it as the naturalizing ground of ideology. It is at this point in Barthes's argument that the French sociologist and semiologist Jean Baudrillard launches his critique of Barthes's semiology, claiming that
in positing a denotative message Barthes succumbs to the most
basic form of ideology. Baudrillard's objections to Barthes's
belief in a denotative photographic message deserve a full ex-
position, for they provide a most powerful tool, not only for
exposing the limitations of Barthes's analysis, but also for un-
covering the economic forces that call into existence such mys-
tifying oppositions as that between connotation and denotation.

Baudrillard, in his first two books, *Le Système des objets* (1968)
and *La Société de consommation* (1970), engages in a critique of
popular culture that is quite similar to Barthes's in *Mythologies,*
deciphering the ideological messages communicated by such
diverse entities as automobiles, contemporary interiors, pop
art, and the leisure industry. But beyond the particular instances of capitalist mystification Baudrillard sees commodities
tending generally to become detached from individual praxis
and abstracted into unidimensional, interchangeable signs of
social status. ("Commodoties" must be considered in the largest
sense of "all goods, services, and activities consumed.") Physical
beauty, for instance, consists not of a harmonious conjunction

of unique features but of a collection of stereotypes generated by the beauty industry that one appropriates by first effacing one's idiosyncratic physical characteristics and then replacing them with standardized signs of beauty sold by the fashion industry in the form of makeup, facials, plastic surgery, wigs, exercise machines, diets, clothes, et cetera. One consumes one's own body and signifies one's social standing through the stereotypes one emulates, but the signs' ultimate function is not to signify anything but to sell merchandise. Commodities, then, constitute a code whose signs exist only to sustain the code; the code regulates both commodities and consumers and thereby integrates consumption with production, completing a circuit of regimentation necessary for the maintenance of late-industrial capitalism.

In *Pour une critique de l'économie politique du signe* (1972), Baudrillard articulates the theoretical principles underlying his earlier books, and here he challenges Barthes's utilization of the connotation/denotation opposition in his analysis of the Panzani advertisement. Only in the context of Baudrillard's larger argument, however, can the full force of his objections to Barthes be appreciated. The central object of Baudrillard's study is the society of consumption, defined as "*that stage where merchandise is immediately produced as sign, as value/sign, and signs (culture) as merchandise.*"[3] To understand properly the collusion of merchandise and signs, claims Baudrillard, one must call into question two misleading analytic oppositions: that between exchange value and usage value in the study of commodities, and that between the signifier and the signified in the study of the sign.

In traditional Marxist economics the usage value of a commodity is its real, objective value as a means for satisfying human needs. Its exchange value is viewed as a deviation from its usage value, a corruption of true value, created by capitalism, that imposes a distance between the commodity and its use. An economic revolution, then, must have as its goal the elimination of exchange value and the establishment of usage value as the sole determinant of a commodity's worth. Such a program Baudrillard finds hopeless, for its assumes the existence of an objective quantum of human needs that can be determined outside a system of exchange. In fact, individual needs are always defined by the social group, which constitutes itself in a system of exchange. Individual needs vary from society to society, and they are delineated by that which exceeds needs. Thus usage value is dependent on exchange value (since it is defined by its opposition to exchange value) and subordinate to it (since usage value and needs are produced by an exchange system). But most important, usage value functions as an *alibi* for exchange value by leaving intact the founding concept of exchange value: value itself. The establishment of a capitalistic economic system depends on the creation of a common denominator among objects and actions, a conceptual abstraction that allows for the equivalence of disparate, polyvalent, contradictory, and discrete entities. Exchange value requires the existence of a code that translates objects and actions into commodities which are interchangeable according to quantitative rules of transformation. Usage value in no way questions this codification of reality into commodities through abstraction, simplification, and reduction. The denunciation of exchange value in the name of usage value thus serves the ends of capitalism by posing as liberation while reconfirming the code upon which exchange value is based.

Baudrillard's critique of the signifier/signified opposition parallels that of the exchange value/usage value opposition. Saussure claims that the relationship between the signifier (acoustic image) and signified (mental concept) is arbitrary, that the sound "cow" has no necessary connection with the concept *cow*, but Baudrillard sees the true arbitrariness of the sign "in the fundamental institution of an exact correlation between some 'discrete' Sa [signifier] and some equally discrete Sé [signified]" (*Critique*, p. 180). The establishment of a logical equivalence between signifier and signified—necessary for the proper functioning of the sign—requires the removal of contradiction from the signified: "The rationality of the sign is founded on the exclusion, on the annihilation of all symbolic ambivalence, to the advantage of a fixed and equational structure" (p. 181). Benveniste's effort to clarify Saussure—by insisting that the relationship between signifier and signified is necessary, while that between signifier and referent (the real world) is arbitrary, and that the signifier-referent relationship lies outside the concern of linguistics—only obscures the controlling power of the signifier and posits an unwarranted division between the signifier and reality: "The essential point is to see that the separation of the sign and the world is a *fiction* and leads to science-fiction. The logic of the equivalence, abstraction, discretion, cutting-out [*découpage*] of the sign includes the Rft [referent] as well as the Sé [signified]—this 'world' which the sign 'evokes' in order better to distance itself is only the *effect* of the sign, its projected shadow, its 'pantographic' projection" (p. 185). Belief in a full reality to which a signifier points is ideological, for the referent involved in the process of signification exists only as an abstract, rational, manipulable counterpart of the signifier. The referent is formed to suit the code—to insure the free exchange of signifiers—and as long as the code exists the referent remains impoverished.

Between the commodity and the linguistic sign lies the photograph—both object (like commodities) and mode of communication (like language). Here Baudrillard attacks the connotation/denotation opposition, with particular reference to Barthes's analysis of the Panzani advertisement. Baudrillard's argument is merely an extension of his critique of the concepts of usage value and the signified; the photograph's nondiscrete, analogical relationship between its signifier and its signified-referent in no way implies the communication of an objective, denotative message since its signified-referent is a commodity-sign already bound inextricably to reductive codes: "Denotation or usage value, objectivity or utility, each is always the complicity of the real with the code under the sign of evidence. And as usage value, the 'literal' and ideal finality of the object resurges continually from the system of exchange value; thus the effect of the concrete, of the real and of denotation arises continually from the complex play of the interference of networks and codes, as white light arises from the interference of the colors of the spectrum. The white light of denotation is nothing more than the play of the spectre of connotations" (p. 193). Barthes recognizes the existence of perceptual, cognitive, and psychological codes that shape reality, and hence the referent of any image, but he posits a virtual denotative dimension of experience that serves as the naturalizing base of the connotative codes. Baudrillard rejects the concept of denotation and argues that connotation, far from being naturalized by denotation, itself naturalizes the codes commonly equated with denotation—codes whose form is the foundation of ideology, which Baudrillard defines as "the seizure of all production (material or symbolic) in an identical process of abstraction, reduction, general equivalence, and exploitation" (p. 177).

The photographic message, its "content," is ideological, since that which is represented is always encoded within an abstract system of signs and commodities, but the photograph's "form," the medium itself (as mass medium), is also ideological, a commodity that is consumed and a sign of an alienated relationship. What characterizes the photograph and other mass media "is that they are antimediators, intransitive, that they manufacture noncommunication—if one agrees to define communication as an *exchange*, as the reciprocal space of a speech and a *response*, hence of a *responsibility*—and not a psychological and moral responsibility, but a personal correlation of one person to another in an exchange" (p. 208). Revolutionaries dream of seizing the mass media and replacing bourgeois messages with egalitarian messages, but the media impose on the recipients of their messages the role of passive, isolated consumers of "a speech without response" (p. 211). Mass media produce messages as factories produce commodities, and as each mass-produced commodity is a copy or representation of an ideal model, so each mass message is created and consumed as a model. Any particular, contextual message, when broadcast by a mass medium, immediately becomes an abstract, mass-distributed, decontextualized sign that combines with other signs broadcast by the medium to form a code. For example, a television crew films an auto workers' strike; when the film is broadcast, the broadcast functions as the sign of the concept "auto workers' strike," "strike in general," "social disturbance," et cetera, and as the sign "news item," interchangeable with other signs/news items in the code "news program."

True communication, by contrast, must be immediate, local and context-specific, a simultaneous and reciprocal exchange between two present parties. That which is communicated must not be univocal or polyvalent (since polyvalence is merely a more complicated relationship between signifiers and signifieds linked by *equivalence*) but *ambivalent*, irreducibly contradictory, *symbolic:* "Only ambivalence (to which we give the acceptation of a rupture of value, of something on this side of or beyond the value/sign, and of an emergence of the symbolic) puts in question the legibility, the false transparence of the sign, its usage value (rational decoding) and its exchange value (the discourse of communication)" (p. 181). The communication model of a one-way transmission of discrete information from a sender to a receiver must be abandoned, for "in the symbolic relation of exchange, there is a simultaneous response, there is neither sender nor receiver on either side of a message, there is no longer a 'message,' that is to say a corpus of information to decipher in a univocal fashion under the aegis of a code. The symbolic consists precisely of breaking that univocity of the 'message,' of restoring the ambivalence of meaning, and of liquidating at the same time the solicitation of the code" (p. 227). Symbolic linguistic exchange disrupts the abstraction of equivalence, and symbolic economic exchange dispenses with the abstraction of value (as in the primitive exchange of gifts described by Marcel Mauss in *Le Don*). Liberated linguistic and economic exchange must destroy the logic of their respective codes, for "the entire repressive and reductive strategy of systems of power is already in the internal logic of the sign, as it is in the internal logic of exchange value and of political economy" (p. 199).

I find convincing Baudrillard's critique of the political economy of the sign, but less so his vision of an unrepressive exchange of goods and signs. After Derrida, talk of *immediate* communication between two *present* parties foregoing the *representation* of a medium must seem suspect, and the implicit primitivism of an exchange of goods outside value (the gift) and of an ambivalent speech (mythological thought) must ultimately surrender to a similar deconstruction. Should not the critique be rejected, then, since the ideal upon which it is founded is compromised? I think not, and it is Barthes who best explains why not in the scattered fragments of his autobiography, *Roland Barthes* (1975).

In his autobiography, Barthes assesses his work as a constant struggle against *Doxa*, or public opinion: the natural, the self-evident, meaning which is transparent and automatic. *Doxa*, like all meaning, is founded in antithesis, "the figure of opposition, the exasperated form of binarism, . . . the very spectacle of meaning."[4] Barthes turns the violence of *Doxa* ("true violence is that of the *self-evident*," p. 85) against itself, utilizing antithesis as "a *theft of language:* I borrow the violence of current discourse for the sake of my own violence, of *meaning-for-myself*" (p. 139). That theft is necessary because "all those—legion—who are outside Power [and *Doxa*] are obliged to steal language" (p. 167). The antithesis Barthes adopts, then, cannot be absolute, but only functional, in service of its critical role. Thus he speaks of denotation as "a scientific myth: that of a 'true' state of language, as if every sentence had inside it an *etymon* (origin and

truth). *Denotation/connotation:* this double concept therefore applies only within the field of truth. Each time I need to test a
message (to demystify it), I subject it to some external instance.
. . . The opposition therefore functions only in the context of a
critical operation analogous to an experiment in chemical
analysis: each time I believe in the truth, I have need of denotation" (p. 67). This truth does not remain fixed, however; an
opposition such as denotation/connotation, or readerly/wri-
terly "is *struck* (like a coinage), but one does not seek to *honor* it.
Then what good is it? Quite simply, it serves *to say something:* it is
necessary to posit a paradigm in order to produce a meaning
and then to be able to divert, to alter it" (p. 92). A utopian
concept thus can serve as one component of an antithesis constructed to demystify the real: "What is a utopia for? To make
meaning. Confronting the present, my present, a utopia is a
second term which permits the sign to function: discourse
about reality becomes possible, I emerge from the aphasia into
which I am plunged by the panic of all that doesn't *work* within
me, in this world which is mine" (p. 76).

Baudrillard's procedure in undermining the denotation/
connotation antithesis is similar to that outlined by Barthes: he
examines a series of oppositions (exchange value/usage value,
signifier/signified, connotation/denotation), which initially
served to demystify *Doxa* but have subsequently assumed the
status of self-evident and natural postulates, and exposes the
complicity between the terms of these antitheses by extracting
the common elements of the oppositions and situating them
within a larger antithesis, whose positive term is the utopia of
immediacy, reciprocity, presence, ambivalence, and the absence of value. That Baudrillard's utopian concepts are vulnerable to critique is not important; as one term of an opposition,
they produce *meaning*—even if it is a meaning directed *against*
meaning (for Baudrillard's attack on the ideology implicit in
the contemporary exchange of goods and signs is ultimately an
attack on all *codes*, on all *systems* of signification).

The position Baudrillard finally occupies is the same as
Barthes's in *Roland Barthes:* that of an enemy of meaning who
must oppose it *within the field of meaning.* Baudrillard and
Barthes reject all forms of mastery, and hence all systems, for
"is it not the characteristic of reality to be *unmasterable?* And is it
not the characteristic of any system to *master* it?" (*Roland Barthes,*
p. 172). Both seek an escape from meaning, but by working

through meaning, not by avoiding it, for *Doxa,* as Barthes points out, is also an escape from meaning in that it represses awareness of the cultural process of meaning's production: "Whence a double tactic: against *Doxa,* one must come out in favor of meaning, for meaning is the product of History, not of Nature; but against Science (paranoiac discourse), one must maintain the utopia of suppressed meaning" (p. 87). Baudrillard's utopian notions allow his critique of the political economy of the sign to emerge, but in *L'Échange symbolique et la mort* (1975) he makes it clear that any return to a primitive society based on symbolic exchange is futile, that one's only option is theoretical violence. Barthes also practices theoretical violence, forming antitheses within systems he seeks to dismantle without succumbing himself to any system: "What then, confronting reality, can one do who rejects mastery? Get rid of the system as apparatus, accept *systematics* as writing" (p. 172).

Barthes sketches in his autobiography a history of his writing as "first of all (mythological *interventions,* then (semiological) *fictions,* then splinters, fragments, *sentences, phrases*" (p. 145)—a series in which a "political and moral obsession is followed by a minor scientific delirium, which in its turn sets off a perverse pleasure (with its undercurrent of fetishism)" (p. 145). The three phases of this history have been outlined here: Barthes's critique of the ideology of a Panzani advertisement fuels semiological reflection on the nature of photographic denotation and connotation and the relationship of this pair to the syntagmatic and paradigmatic aspects of the photographic code; the existence of a denotative syntagmatic order proves to be a fiction; and Baudrillard's analysis of the ideology of denotation calls into question the repressive force of all codification, thus instituting the fragmenting practice of theoretical violence that Barthes directs toward the creation of pleasure without domination. Yet this history must be considered not a narrative of error's abolition but the delineation of a field of activity, for moral intervention, semiological delirium, and perverse violence are all necessary endeavors. Utopias of an escape from meaning, of ambivalence and the end of value, will not soon terminate men's will to power that manifests itself in systems of mastery, and as important as utopian visions are for undoing ideology political action must also proceed by the establishment of denaturalizing oppositions within repressive codes and by the erection of competitive systems that dislocate the structures of *Doxa*'s power. The cultural critic cannot dispense with codes, nor would he want to, for as Barthes observes, "Structure at least affords me two terms, one of which I can deliberately choose and the other dismiss; hence it is on the whole a (modest) pledge of freedom" (*Roland Barthes*, p. 117)—a freedom he loses when immersed in cacophony or silence. Hence Barthes concludes that his text "is in fact *readerly:* I am on the side of structure, of the sentence, of the sentenced text" (p. 92). The same must be said of Baudrillard, whose attack on reductive logical codes proceeds by a most lucid logic.

In *Elements of Semiology* (1964) Barthes admiringly cites as a model for characterizing all semiological codes Saussure's comparison of the articulation of signification and value in a linguistic system to cutting shapes from a sheet of paper, one side of which represents the signifier, the other the signified, whose pieces derive their meaning from their relationship to one another. Baudrillard argues that ideology resides less in the cuts made in the paper than in the reduction of reality to the thickness of a single sheet of paper. If Baudrillard were to adopt Barthes's comparison in *S/Z* of the network of codes to the stars in the sky, he would describe the codes as the cartographic projection of an infinite and unmasterable space. Barthes would no doubt agree. Yet Barthes still traces shapes in that sky, as he says in *S/Z*, "like the soothsayer drawing on it with the tip of his staff an imaginary rectangle wherein to consult, according to certain principles, the flight of birds."[5] In *Roland Barthes* he clarifies the significance of this metaphor: "it must have been a fine thing to see, in those days: that staff marking out the sky, the one thing that cannot be marked; then, too, any such gesture is mad: solemnly to trace a limit of which immediately *nothing* is left, except for the intellectual remnance of a cutting out, to devote oneself to the totally ritual and totally arbitrary preparation of a meaning" (p. 47). With his staff he delineates codes, and with antitheses he intervenes politically: "Like a magician's wand, the concept, especially if it is coupled [with its antithesis], *raises* a possibility of writing: here, he [Barthes] said, lies the power of saying something" (*Roland Barthes*, p. 110). The soothsayer's staff, the magician's wand: ephemeral yet necessary tools that mark nothing but allow something to be said.

1. Reprinted in Roland Barthes, *Image/Music/Text,* trans. Stephen Heath (New York: Hill and Wang, 1979), pp. 32–51. All subsequent quotations from this volume will be cited in the text. Throughout my essay I cite, whenever possible, readily available translations of Barthes's work.

2. Roland Barthes, *Mythologies,* trans. and comp. Annette Lavers (New York: Hill and Wang, 1972), p. 131.

3. Jean Baudrillard, *Pour une critique de l'économie politique du signe* (Paris: Gallimard, 1972), p. 178. All translations of *Critique* are my own; all subsequent quotations from *Critique* will be cited in the text.

4. *Roland Barthes,* trans. Richard Howard (New York: Hill and Wang, 1977), p. 138. Subsequent quotations from *Roland Barthes* will be cited in the text.

5. Roland Barthes, *S/Z,* trans. Richard Miller (New York: Hill and Wang, 1974), p. 14.

Women and
Ideology

Women and Revolution—Their Theories, Our Experience

Angelika Bammer
University of Wisconsin–Madison

Yes, there are a lot of factors dividing women from each other—
class, caste, religion, race, education (or the lack of it), one's field
of work (in the house or out of it) and many other complex
historical forces. Yet if we look at the nature and basis of women's
oppression, we discover that our sex determines our common
predicament in a very fundamental way.

—from the editorial of the first issue (January 1979) of *Manushi:
A Journal about Women and Society*, India's first feminist journal

IN her autobiographical *Reminiscences of Lenin* Clara Zetkin
recalls a discussion with Lenin in 1920 on what Marxists had
officially come to call "the Woman Question." After criticizing
Zetkin for permitting women in the German Communist Party
to support the organizing efforts of prostitutes rather than
educating proletarian women in the "correct" consciousness
and the "correct" revolutionary goals, Lenin continued: "They
tell me that in your women's meetings the readings and discus-
sions center around questions of sexuality and marriage . . .
that these are your major concerns. I couldn't believe it. We are
struggling against counterrevolution all over the world. . . .
And meanwhile our women are talking about sexuality and
marital issues!"[1] But, argued Zetkin, these *are* revolutionary
issues, certainly for women.

143

Lenin's response, that a period of intensive class struggle is not the time to focus on questions of women's sexuality or personal relationships, is congruent with the orthodox Marxist position defining women's oppression as a "secondary contradiction" subordinate to the "primary contradiction" of class. It illustrates that the concerns of women are not necessarily perceived as revolutionary by those who define "the Revolution." This presents a dilemma for those who, like Zetkin, recognize that for women a revolution would require not only a change in economic class structures but a fundamental transformation of patriarchal culture. For unless the specificity of women's oppression under patriarchy is as central a focus of radical analyses and activism as class oppression, we will be left with "a social revolution which would leave male leadership and control essentially untouched."[2] For women, not much would have changed.

Revolution is not a mechanical rotation of the wheel of power. The very axis around which revolve positions of power and powerlessness must be broken if we are to go beyond their mere reversal to effect their ultimate dissolution. More far-reaching than any revolution, such a transformation of social and cultural structures would ultimately create a new kind of human being as human consciousness underwent fundamental changes. "Thinking itself," says Adrienne Rich, "will be transformed."[3] In this process literary texts, with their power to capture the imagination and affect the way we perceive ourselves and the world around us, can play a significant role.

The choices made in a text—what is said, how it is said, and (often most significantly) what is not said—inevitably have an ideological function. But rarely does this become more evident than in the political sensitivities of a period of social upheaval. The history of texts by women who wrote about women within the context of a society undergoing radical structural changes might, therefore, give us a particularly acute insight into the relationship between class revolution and what Robin Morgan, in her poem *Monster,* dreams of as "a women's revolution."[4] How have women asked "the Woman Question"? How do their texts describe the material conditions of women's lives? Where do they locate the source(s) of oppression, the contradiction(s), the basis of change? And finally, how have these texts been treated within the revolution of which they were a part?

We find, not surprisingly, that texts which view the processes of social change from the specific vantage point of women have—like women themselves—been treated as secondary in the context of revolutionary culture. They have been scorned for their attention to what were officially considered the trivialities of personal problems at a time of more pressing concerns or even maligned as agents of "false consciousness." To speak as a woman was considered dissident. Censorship, operating on every conceivable level, setting in before a writer ever committed her thoughts to paper and continuing through the erasure of her words from the records of literary history, has silenced countless women's "dissident" voices. As a result, the number of texts by women that raise issues out of line with the goals and strategy of those who orchestrated "the Revolution" is very small. Probably few were ever written, fewer survived, and fewer still are actually available to us in print, in translation, in libraries or archives. Yet in the wake of feminist scholarship those texts which do exist are being rediscovered, reprinted, reevaluated. Writers like Alexandra Kollontai, Christa Wolf, or Shih Ming are being (re)claimed as part of women's cultural and political history as feminist critics lay bare the traces of patriarchal ideology inscribed in the history of literature and academic scholarship.

In the early 1970s renewed critical attention was brought to a writer whose outspoken feminism had placed her in the center of political controversy during the early years of the Soviet Revolution. But several decades of silence had almost erased Alexandra Kollontai from women's history when activist feminist scholars in Britain, notably the historian Sheila Rowbotham, caused her theoretical and fictional writings to be reissued. In this restoration some of Kollontai's texts—her autobiography (which had never before been published in its original, unexpurgated version), her fictional writings (which had never appeared in English in their entirety)—were accessible to us for the first time.[5]

The treatment of Alexandra Kollontai and of her writings illustrates the tenuous position of a woman who refuses to subordinate women's liberation to class struggle. "Why should women's matters be considered any less important than other things?" asks the narrator of *Vasilisa Malygina*.[6] Kollontai's commitment to the Soviet Revolution was never questioned. Yet her writings on the issue of women's sexual and emotional oppression became the subject of heated debate and ridicule within the Soviet Communist Party. In *Love of Worker Bees*, which was published in 1923 as part of a series devoted to "Revolution in Feelings and Morality," Kollontai shows that until women are free of the institutionalized and internalized repression of their sexuality, reproductive freedom, and selfhood, a revolution will not only be incomplete but impossible. In Kollontai's short story "Sisters," a woman recounting the brief years of her marriage comes to realize that the revolution to which she and her husband, as comrades, had dedicated themselves has somehow passed her by. One night, when her husband brings home a prostitute, she suddenly understands that this revolution has not made women free. Still dependent on the power of men, the two women—wife and prostitute alike—share a common fate. "It suddenly dawned on me," she realizes, "that if I hadn't had a husband, I would have been in the same position as her."[7] While Party leaders protested that it was embarrassing "to be forever looking under the bedsheets,"[8] Kollontai insisted that "without realigning sexual and family relationships in a new . . . way, the new socio-economic system will soon come to resemble the old."[9]

Progressive Marxist thinkers, then as now, have recognized that the feminist analyses of a Kollontai or a Zetkin are not only not incompatible with Marxism but embody the very essence of a dialectical-materialist method. However, when political leaders established in positions of authority become cautious maintainers of the existing order, official policy tends to be pronounced in the voice of orthodoxy. And it was the cultural and political orthodoxy of a revolution in retrenchment that determined Kollontai's fate. Within a decade of its publication, *Love of Worker Bees* was being invoked as a "model of 'petit-bourgeois debauchery,' a judgment which ensured it never reached the audience for which it was intended."[10] As her autobiography reveals, Kollontai herself had recognized early on "how little our Party concerned itself with the fate of the women of the working class and how meagre was its interest in women's liberation."[11] When *The Autobiography of a Sexually Emancipated Communist Woman* was published in 1926, this passage, like many other references to her feminist activity, had been deleted. Kollontai, like her texts, was silenced. In 1924 she had been sent into diplomatic exile to Norway.

The East German novelist Christa Wolf offers a more contemporary example of the reaction of cultural policy makers to a woman who refuses to ignore the contradictions in the lives of women that even socialism does not resolve. Wolf's novel *The Quest for Christa T.* was published in the German Democratic Republic in 1968 in the atmosphere of open political debate that had developed during the preceding years of political and economic stabilization often referred to, from a Western perspective, as "the thaw." Like Kollontai, Wolf describes her society and its changes from the perspective of a woman. Her protagonist, Christa T., meets a young woman who works as a streetcar conductor and at home is regularly beaten and raped by her husband; she is now in the hospital for her third abortion. Suddenly Christa T. realizes that the everyday reality of this woman's life has not been changed by the grand historical scheme of socialist revolution and that "when she reads the paper, it never occurs to her that what they say has anything to do with her."[12] She has been forgotten. Against this indifference, Christa T. pits her impassioned demand that "help must be brought to all, now."[13]

Wolf problematizes the dialectic of the individual "I" and the collective "we." As long as a woman is not allowed to establish her identity as an autonomous self, how can she participate in the creation of a truly collective society? As Christa T. undertakes the "long and seemingly endless journey to find herself,"[14] she loses that self among the old expectations of wifehood and motherhood and the new demands of socialist citizenhood. Wolf recognizes that the process of learning to say "I" is as difficult as it is essential for those who have been denied recognition as historical subjects. Her consequent insistence on the need, particularly for women, to validate individual subjectivity caused Wolf's novel to become the focus of considerable controversy and the target of political censure. For women in the German Democratic Republic, the goal of socialist perfection was still a very distant one, and Wolf reminded government leaders of the work that remained to be done. Her reminder was uncomfortable. Published initially only in a very limited edition (which went out of print almost immediately), *The Quest for Christa T.* was officially pulled out of circulation for the next five years. Although this decree made Wolf's text inaccessible to women in her own country, it was widely published and translated in the West soon after its appearance, and women responded with enthusiasm. Caught in the confusion of changing values, they recognized in Christa T. their own struggle to act, to define themselves as subjects in society. Wolf's recognition of "the difficulty of saying 'I'" that punctuates *The Quest for Christa T.* reverberated in the consciousness of her female readers.

When the concerns of women are ignored, censured, or silenced as irrelevant or even harmful to "the Revolution," the relationship between women's liberation and class revolution becomes problematic. What are the implications for women when the two are separated? This is the question raised by Kollontai, by Wolf, and, again, by the Chinese writer Shih Ming. An activist student leader in the revolutionary movement in China during the 1920s, Shih Ming began writing consciously political fiction in the 1930s when Chiang Kai-shek's attempt to reimpose Confucianism intensified the ideological battles between the warring parties. The years of political and cultural upheaval following the May Fourth student demonstrations in 1919 had witnessed widespread feminist activity in China. The student movement had propelled many young women into radical politics, and women writers were speaking out about the conditions of Chinese women's lives. As Ibsen's Nora became a symbol of women's revolt, a lecture by Lu Hsun at Peking Women's University in 1923 asking, "What happens after Nora slams the door?" drew national attention to the revolutionary significance of feminist issues.

In the course of the 1930s, however, pressing economic needs led Communist Party leaders to rank women's liberation as a lesser priority, and within a decade feminist demands were rebuffed altogether. In 1942 an editorial for International Women's Day by the nationally known writer Ting Ling appeared in the Yenan *Liberation Daily* criticizing Party leaders for their lack of attention to the continuing oppression of Chinese women. Official response was unequivocal. Ting Ling was censured and the Party decreed that "'full sex equality had already been established' and that . . . feminism was outdated and harmful."[15] It is not surprising, therefore, that women writing of women's experience during these years of revolutionary struggles are largely unknown to us. What happened to women like Ping Hsin, author of a volume of essays, *On Women*, or Ling Shu-hua, who published a collection of short stories, *Women*, in 1930? Who has heard of Lu Ying or Hsin Pinyin?[16] Where are their texts? Only fragments are available to us; little has been translated. Shih Ming, whose pseudonym ("Lost Name") has the ring of historical irony, has been almost completely forgotten.

One of Shih Ming's stories, however, was restored to us in a collection of Third World writings about women published in 1973.[17] "Fragment from a Lost Diary" is the story of a young woman who, like Shih Ming herself, has been active in the revolutionary student movement. The narrative takes place in 1925, in the days preceding the historic and violent demonstration in Shanghai that sparked the May Thirtieth Movement, the first nationwide mass resistance against imperialism in China. In diary form, the protagonist, who remains nameless, records the experiences that lead her to conclude, in her final entry: "Woman and revolution—strange pair" (p. 224). Confined to her bed by a nauseous pregnancy and, finally, by an agonizing and possibly fatal abortion, she is completely cut off from the revolution she herself helped set in motion. Like Christa T., she begins to question her social identity: "Laid away like this, a dead one, is it possible for me to feel the same sense of value, to believe in my own significance as a social being, as I do when living with the working masses?" (p. 219). "Weighed down by a stone" (p. 224), her pregnant body has become the instrument of her destruction, for as the revolution mobilizes she, the revolutionary, is immobilized by the demands of reproduction. "What small regard the female womb has for the historic necessities!" she exclaims. "It is its own history and its own necessity. It is the dialectic reduced to its simplest statement" (p. 211). If dialectics, as defined by Marxist theory, is "the study of contradiction *in the very essence of objects*"[18] then "woman" and "revolution," suggests "Fragment from a Lost Diary," are antithetical forces.

Indeed they are, if we interpret their relationship from within a theoretical model that defines the "public" sphere of production as the primary locus of oppression and, consequently, of revolutionary action while relegating emotional and biological reproduction to a separate sphere defined as "private" and, therefore, secondary. Kollontai, Wolf, and Shih Ming were writing within the ideological context of precisely such a model—the Marxian theory of social change as the process of class struggle. Change, says Mao, can only come about when individuals understand the contradictions inherent in social processes. But, he insists "none of this knowledge can be acquired apart from activity in production."[19] The solution to "the Woman Question" proposed by Lenin in *Women and Society*, that "in order to achieve the complete emancipation of women . . . we must have social economy and the participation of women in general productive labor,"[20] follows logically from these premises. For women, however, this is a solution only in part.

Feminists, from within a Marxist tradition,[21] have argued that a narrowly economistic model of revolution based on concepts of class and production that ignore the significantly different conditions of men and women in society is both insufficient and imprecise. Applied dogmatically, it even becomes dangerous. Descriptions of women in revolutionary societies illustrate some of the problems that result when women try to conform to a male-defined strategy of social change. Kollontai dutifully[22] expurgates her autobiography, before it becomes public, of the very statements that express the most fundamental goals of her revolutionary activity, "the complete liberation of the working woman and the creation of a new sexual morality."[23] Wolf's Christa T. torments herself with guilt that her contradictions are inadequate to the needs of the new socialist society to which she is committed. If, as a former student of hers proclaims, "it is those who fit in who are healthy,"[24] then indeed it is she who is sick. Christa T. doubts herself, not the structures that define her, and the narrative ends with her death. The protagonist of "Fragment from a Lost Diary" feels that she is not only useless, but superfluous, a burden to herself and her comrades and an obstacle in the path of social progress. Sacrificing her dream of motherhood to the revolution by aborting the child she had secretly desired, she wonders, in self-contempt, whether her own death would not be her most meaningful contribution.

As they participate in a revolution that reflects the needs and interests of men and often forgets or ignores the specific needs and interests of women, these women are caught within a fundamental contradiction: while their self-denial is praised as service to "the greater cause," their self-affirmation is likely to be punished as betrayal. The historical difficulty of developing a feminist theory—witnessed by its virtual absence in revolutionary societies, by the distrust and avoidance of theory which, until recently, has characterized much of American feminism, and by the ambivalent struggle of European feminism to both relate to and free itself from its Marxist base—is an indication of the seriousness of this dilemma. It must be confronted, however, for self-denial is not revolutionary: it is self-destructive. A theory and practice of revolution are only possible, maintains a dialectical-materialist method, if they are grounded in our experience of material reality. To deny or distort that experience thus deprives us of the very possibility of revolutionary action.

Implicit in the position that conception arises out of perception lies a basic and significant assumption about the nature of theory itself. For if the source of our theory is our experience of reality, then theory is inherently subjective. Its inevitable blind spot can only be identified by those who acknowledge that subjectivity. Therefore, concludes Adrienne Rich, as long as men "still live in the unacknowledged cave of their own subjectivity, their denied fears and longings,"[25] we cannot expect a male-engineered revolution to abolish the oppression of women. The problem is not that men, from where they stand, are unable to see women and their concerns (or see us merely peripherally), but that they claim objectivity and universality for their perspective. To deny the validity of that claim is thus the first step out of women's dilemma. For we can no longer afford to remain unseen or to distance ourselves from our own experience in order to be recognized within the male line of vision. Instead, we must recast the model of revolution from our perspective, developing a theory and a practice out of an understanding of the historical reality of women's lives.

Alexandra Kollontai, Christa Wolf, and Shih Ming point to the need for such a model but do not present us with a blueprint for the perfect revolution. Unlike Lenin, they refuse to prescribe a simple answer to "the Woman Question." Instead they describe the lives of women, their problems, their dreams, their needs. Solutions remain implicit, imbedded in the recognition that the specificity of women's revolutionary practice will evolve, ineluctably, from the specificity of women's experience. It is the truthfulness with which these texts articulate that experience which has made them, as Sheila Rowbotham said of Kollontai, "peculiarly heretical, peculiarly embarrassing, peculiarly relevant, and particularly revolutionary."[26]

An exploration of the nature of women's experience inevitably seems to lead to one question that has alternately been decried as heretical or proclaimed as revolutionary—the question of difference between women and men. In the context of a socialist structure, organized around the premise of common goals defined by common interests, the acknowledgment of difference becomes particularly problematic even while its consequences impair the functioning of that structure. Knowing, however, that, for women, it is the denial of difference that has had the most serious consequence, forcing men to deny that women even exist or have a right to be, Kollontai, Wolf, and Shih Ming take the risk of exploring this question. They describe the crippling effects of unspoken difference on human interaction when women, struggling to communicate experience that is not shared, fall into the gap of silence that separates them from the men with whom they live and work. Absorbed in concerns of their own, the men—the husbands of Christa T. and Vasilisa Malygina, the mate of the woman in "Fragment from a Lost Diary"—are unable to hear what the women are thus unable to tell them.

This silence is broken only when women speak to one another and recognize the bonds that have always connected them. Not until the pregnant woman in Shih Ming's story meets Dr. Li, a woman who shares with her the agony of bearing children who must die in a time of warfare and starvation, are they both able to speak of the pain they, as women, must suffer. As Kollontai's Vasilisa Malygina speaks to her woman friend, Grusha, she realizes that the intimacy she had struggled vainly to create in her marriage grows easily in their friendship and that it is Grusha with whom she will "live and work, work and fight, live and love life."[27] And in The Quest for Christa T. the lives of the protagonist, the narrator, and even, in its autobiographical nature, of the author herself, become inseparable as the voices of all three women are woven into a single narrative fabric.

While it is relatively easy to establish difference between men and women as a material, historical fact, to venture beyond fact and explore its sources is a much more difficult and dangerous undertaking, for it threatens basic assumptions on which patriarchal culture has been erected. Kollontai, at least in her fiction, does not pursue the question of causes but instead looks toward a future in which the complete liberation of women will have overcome the effects of social difference. In the meantime, change is a process of "action, work, struggle,"[28] and, as the young Zhenya in Kollontai's "Three Generations" reminds us in the final words of the narrative: "we have so much work to do!"[29] In The Quest for Christa T. Christa Wolf approaches the

issue of sexual and gender difference tentatively, almost anx-
iously. Several years later she is less cautious. In "Self-
Experiment," a fantastic tale of a scientific experiment that
transforms a woman into a man,[30] difference is inscribed even
in the name ("Anders") chosen by this woman-become-man.
Wolf suggests that not only do men and women inhabit different bodies and speak a different language, but that, having
once given up their human sensitiveness in return for the
privileges of power, men have ceased to be fully human. Mil-
lennia of lived difference have thus become virtually insur-
mountable as historical gender has become our sexual identity.

In "Fragment from a Lost Diary," Shih Ming tears through
this shell of social gender that, in the course of history, has
grown into our bodies like a garment worn too long. Shih Ming
discovers, beneath gender, the very essence of difference and
locates the sexual center of difference in the body itself. The
ideological implications of such a position, in theory and in
practice, are enormous. If we recognize our body as a basic
component of our material reality, then women's experience of
sexuality and the processes of reproduction constitutes a basis
of knowledge that is, essentially and fundamentally, different
from that of men. If this is true, if men thus cannot know what
women know, then on the level of theory the entire foundation
of patriarchal authority is unhinged. On the level of practice,
the consequences are equally profound. For through our socially assigned roles and our biologically defined potential,
women, unlike men, have been reproducers as well as pro-
ducers. Our bodies have been the nexus of the spheres of reproduction and production. The interlocking systems of economic and sexual exploitation within patriarchal culture, the
connections and conflicts between women's dual role in the
world of work and in the institution of the family, thus constitute the principal contradiction for women that forms the basis
of a feminist analysis. Consequently, if the contradictions experienced by men are necessarily different from those experienced by women, our revolutionary practice must also be different, for, as Mao himself insisted, "qualitatively different
contradictions can only be resolved by qualitatively different
methods."[31]

In her exploration of the experience and institution of
motherhood, Adrienne Rich gives us a glimpse of the theoretical and practical implications of a model of revolutionary

transformation based on a materialist and historical analysis of
the particularity of women's experience and the contradictions
inherent in that experience. Rich's conclusion, that "the repos-
session by women of our bodies will bring far more essential
change to human society than the seizing of the means of production by workers,"[32] is a radical feminist challenge to a male-
defined revolution.

Ideology is inscribed in literary texts as well as in literary
judgments. Our perception of the aesthetic value and the historical significance of a text will thus necessarily be affected by
our own position, by the degree, for example, to which we have
either a vested interest in patriarchy or a commitment to feminism. The seeming contradictions between variant readings often merely reveal ideological differences, and a simple realign-
ment of our critical theory from a male-centered to a feminist
perspective can fundamentally alter the meaning of a text.
Texts which were judged insignificant can suddenly acquire
particular significance; texts which were hailed as revolutionary
are no longer necessarily so. Writers like Alain Robbe-Grillet,
Günter Grass, Norman Mailer, or Charles Bukowski, for example, have been celebrated by a new literary left as fighters
against an oppressive cultural ideology. Yet when they uncriti-
cally indulge in narrations of physical and psychological violence against women, they are certainly not fighting against the
oppression of women. And should it really surprise us that
their concept of revolution leaves patriarchal power structures
intact, "for patriarchy . . . is still *their* order, confirming them in
privilege."[33] These writers are radical only in the eyes of the
brothers they imply as readers. Radical, we must ask, for
whom?

Such a question enables us to recognize the importance of
such texts as *Love of Worker Bees, The Quest for Christa T.,* and
"Fragment from a Lost Diary." As we perceive the congruence
between the issues raised in these texts and the issues confronting women in society, they shift from the fringes of a male-
defined revolutionary culture to the very center of women's
radical challenge to patriarchal structures. Revolutionary
theory and practice based on men's experience have effectively
placed women outside of history, reducing us—as Kollontai,
Wolf, and Shih Ming illustrate—to mere objects of historical
forces. By making women's experience visible, by recording the
fragments of our lives that are revealed as we begin to break

our silence, by thus validating our existence and our concerns, texts which speak of women's experience from a woman's perspective are engaged in the ongoing process of transformation in which women are becoming subjects of our own history. It is in this sense that these texts, for women, are profoundly revolutionary.

Postscript

LENINGRAD. Three women who contributed to the Soviet dissident community's first underground feminist magazine, *Women and Russia,* have been detained and warned they will be arrested if another issue appears.

—from *Her Say,* quoted in *off our backs* 10, no. 3 (March 1980)

1. Clara Zetkin, *Erinnerungen an Lenin* (Berlin: Dietz, 1957), p. 65. This (nonliteral) translation is my own. Although Zetkin's text has appeared as *Reminiscences of Lenin,* it is usually titled *Lenin on the Woman Question.* This latter title, which implicitly attributes to Lenin what Zetkin has written, is an ironic reminder of the very attitude of appropriation against which Zetkin was fighting.

2. Adrienne Rich, *Of Woman Born: Motherhood as Experience and Institution* (New York: Bantam Books, 1977), p. 100.

3. Ibid., p. 292.

4. Robin Morgan, *Monster* (New York: Vintage Books, 1972), p. 82.

5. Alexandra Kollontai wrote her *Autobiography of a Sexually Emancipated Communist Woman* in 1926. The fact that, even in its politically "cleaned-up" version, it was initially not published in the Soviet Union but in Germany (in German), and that the first uncensored edition was again a translation (into English), is an indication of the controversial nature of this text. Kollontai's novel had been translated in 1927 as *Red Love* and again in 1931 as *Free Love.* It was not until 1978, however, that this novel, now entitled *Vasilisa Malygina,* and the two accompanying short stories, "Sisters" and "Three Generations," were published in their entirety in English as *Love of Worker Bees,* trans. Cathy Porter (Chicago: Cassandra Editions, 1978).

6. Kollontai, *Love of Worker Bees,* p. 22.

7. Ibid., p. 220.

8. Sheila Rowbotham, "Alexandra Kollontai: Woman's Liberation and Revolutionary Love," *The Spokesman,* June 1970, p. 30.

9. Germaine Greer, Foreword to Kollontai, *The Autobiography of a Sexually Emancipated Communist Woman* (London: Orbach & Chambers, 1978), p. xii.

10. Cathy Porter, Introduction to Kollontai, *Love of Worker Bees,* p. 16.

11. Kollontai, *Autobiography,* p. 13.

12. Christa Wolf, *Nachdenken über Christa T.* (Neuwied/Berlin: Luchterhand, 1971), p. 165. All translations from this text are my own.

13. Ibid., p. 165.

14. Ibid., p. 222.

15. Delia Davin, *Woman-Work: Women and the Party in Revolutionary China* (New York: Oxford University Press, 1979), p. 36.

16. For further discussion of women writing in China during this period see Yi-Tsi Feuerwerker, "Women as Writers in the 1920's and 1930's," in *Women in Chinese Society,* ed. Roxanne Witke and Margery Wolf (Stanford, Calif.: Stanford University Press, 1975).

17. Shih Ming, "Fragment from a Lost Diary," in *Fragment from a Lost Diary,* ed. Naomi Katz and Nancy Milton (Boston: Beacon Press, 1975). Further references to this work will be cited in parentheses in the text.

18. Mao Tse-tung, "On Contradiction," in *Four Essays on Philosophy* (Peking: Foreign Languages Press, 1968), p. 23. Mao is quoting Lenin.

19. Mao, "On Practice," in *Four Essays on Philosophy,* p. 2.

20. Quoted in *The Woman Question* (New York: International Publishers, 1951), p. 52.

21. Zillah Eisenstein, Nancy Hartsock, Ann Foreman, Nancy Chodorow, Gayle Rubin, Rayna Reiter, Dorothy Smith, Juliet Mitchell, Annette Kuhn, and Sheila Rowbotham are only some of the Marxist feminists currently writing and publishing in English.

22. If we recognize and respect Kollontai's loyalty to the Communist Party, we must give her the credit of assuming that the self-censorship of her writings was voluntary.

23. Kollontai, *Autobiography,* pp. 47–48.

24. Wolf, *Christa T.,* p. 141.

25. Rich, *Of Woman Born,* p. 69.

26. Rowbotham, "Alexandra Kollontai," p. 32.

27. Kollontai, *Love of Worker Bees,* p. 181.

28. Ibid., p. 222.

29. Ibid., p. 211.

30. Christa Wolf, "Selbstversuch," in *Unter den Linden* (Berlin/Weimar: Aufbau Verlag, 1974).

31. Mao, "On Contradiction," p. 38.

32. Rich, *Of Woman Born,* p. 292.

33. Ibid., p. 69.

The Semiotic Functions of Ideology in Literary Discourse

Diane Griffin Crowder

Cornell College

L ITERARY criticism has been divided historically into two major approaches with conflicting views on the nature of literature. One group of critics has viewed literature as a mimetic representation of a reality outside the text. These critics assume a direct correspondence between the linguistic signs that compose the text and their referents in the real world. Such ideological criticisms evaluate the text upon its adequacy as a representation of some aspect of reality: economics for the Marxist, psychology for the Freudian, and so on. Critics of the other group focus their attention on the structures of the text itself, ignoring its relationship to the sociocultural context. With greater or lesser degrees of scientific rigor, they dissect it to describe its internal operations, and often deny the relationship between literature and the outside world. Ideology rarely receives much attention from such critics.

This admittedly simplistic division of critical thought has become increasingly problematic in the past twenty years for three reasons. First, abstractionism in literature calls into question the traditional mimetic function of literature. In highly experimental texts it is often fatuous to ask whether the work gives an adequate expression to external reality, since it makes no attempt to do so.

Yet one finds increasing rejection of purely formalist approaches, because such critical models fail to account for the undeniable fact that readers attempt to correlate texts with their perceptions of reality. As Riffaterre has noted, the reader interprets even the most abstract text as though it meant to convey a message about the real world.[1] If frustrated in this expectation of mimesis, the reader is likely to reject the text as nonliterary nonsense.

Finally, the emergence of feminist criticism in the past decade has placed a great strain on this historical dichotomy. Like other ideological criticisms, feminist criticism demands a critical model to account for the relationship between the text and the world. The feminist critic examines the portrayal of women in literature and compares it to the sociohistorical position of real women in culture, thereby assuming a correspondence between language and reality. But, unlike other ideological criticisms, feminism assumes that the language itself, as well as literary forms, is a repository of patriarchal ideology, and seeks a model for the analysis of formal linguistic and literary structures. A theory of literature that transcends this historical dichotomy is needed in order to account for such texts as Wittig's *Les Guérillères*,[2] which explicitly combines a radical critique and restructuring of linguistic and literary codes with ideological messages intended to restructure the reader's perception of reality.

I propose a critical model based upon semiotic principles as the only means to overcome the limitations of both mimetic and formalist theories. Since the central issue dividing critics concerns the relationship between literature and reality, text and sociohistorical context, this critical model must contain a conceptual means of comparing apples and oranges: that is, of equating the linguistic signs and formal structures of literature with the culture in which literature is produced and consumed.

The central notion of semiotics is the idea that the world is a complex set of interrelated sign systems. This concept provides a way out of the dilemma. If cultural reality is itself a set of sign systems, the relationship between literary discourse and reality is a relationship between sign systems, presumably governed by semiotic principles. The two approaches to literary criticism can therefore be subsumed into a general theory of the relationships between signs and sign systems.

While crucial to the solution of the literary problem, this conceptual shift in itself does not constitute the whole answer. Indeed, each time it has been proposed, it has been rejected by ideologically oriented critics as a "trick" by which semiotic critics can pretend to deal with questions of ideology when in fact literary semiotics to date has been largely formalist in nature.[3] Semioticians have attained a semblance of scientific objectivity by generally ignoring the problem of ideology in literary discourse. Wittig has noted that semiotics, in theory, holds great promise for reconciling formalist descriptions with rigorous analysis of the relationships between texts and ideologies. But she has rightly accused semiotic critics of hedging on the question of ideology by abstracting literature from specific social concerns and pretending that sign systems have no ideological value.[4] As a science of signs, semiotics has so far failed to provide a valid model for feminist criticism.[5]

I use feminist criticism as my example because, more clearly than any other ideology, feminism is itself predicated upon the perception of the semiotic status of the link between sign vehicles and sign functions, signifiers and signifieds. Feminism poses two axioms. First, that biological sex—the signifier—does not account for the complex superstructure of codes that determine our definitions of gender—the signified. The relationship between being biologically female and being defined as "woman" or "feminine" is a semiotic relationship. Semiotics would therefore seem ideally suited to feminist critics.

But feminism has a second axiom that so far has not appeared as a primary concept in semiotic literary theory. For feminists, the noncausal—hence symbolic—nature of the relationship between biological sex and culturally determined gender codes leads to the conclusion that the encoding of gender into cultural sign systems is governed by ideological principles. The signs of our culture are presumed not to be innocent forms, but to serve the goals of masculinist ideology.

It is this distinction between feminism and other ideologies that deserves attention. For feminists, it is not only the messages of literature that serve ideological ends. Sexist ideology is present in the very structures of the verbal and nonverbal codes from which messages are constructed.[6] In *Les Guérillères* Wittig's collective female narrator presents a clearly semiotic analysis of the problem posed by this all-pervasive ideology:

> Elles disent, malheureuse, ils t'ont chassée du monde des signes, et cependant ils t'ont donné des noms, ils t'ont appelée esclave, toi malheureuse esclave. Comme des maîtres ils ont exercé leur droit de maître. Ils écrivent de ce droit de donner des noms qu'il va si loin que l'on peut considérer l'origine du langage comme un acte d'autorité émanant de ceux qui dominent. Ainsi ils disent qu'ils ont dit, ceci est telle ou telle chose, ils ont attaché à un objet et à un fait

tel vocable et par là ils se les ont pour ainsi dire appropriés. Elles
disent, ce faisant ils ont gueulé hurlé de toutes leurs forces pour te
réduire au silence. Elles disent, le langage que tu parles t'em-
poisonne la glotte la langue le palais les lèvres. Elles disent le langage que tu parles est fait de mots qui te tuent. Elles disent, le
langage que tu parles est fait de signes qui à proprement parler
désignent ce qu'ils se sont appropriés. Ce sur quoi ils n'ont pas mis
la main, ce sur quoi ils n'ont pas fondu comme des rapaces aux yeux
multiples, cela n'apparaît pas dans le langage que tu parles. Cela se
manifeste juste dans l'intervalle que les maîtres n'ont pas pu com-
bler avec leurs mots de propriétaires et de possesseurs, cela peut se
chercher dans la lacune, dans tout ce qui n'est pas la continuité de
leurs discours, dans le zéro, le O, le cercle parfait que tu inventes
pour les emprisonner et pour les vaincre. [Pp. 162–64]

[The women say, unhappy one, men have expelled you from the
world of symbols [signs] and yet have given you names, they have
called you slave, you unhappy slave. Masters, they have exercised
their rights as masters. They write, of their authority to accord
names, that it goes back so far that the origin of language itself may
be considered an act of authority emanating from those who domi-
nate. Thus they say that they have said, this is such or such a thing,
they have attached a particular word to an object or a fact and
thereby consider themselves to have appropriated it. The women
say, so doing the men have bawled shouted with all their might to
reduce you to silence. The women say, the language you speak
poisons your glottis tongue palate lips. They say, the language you
speak is made up of signs that rightly speaking designate what men
have appropriated. Whatever they have not laid hands on, whatever they have not pounced on like many-eyed birds of prey, does
not appear in the language you speak. This is apparent precisely in
the intervals that your masters have not been able to fill with their
words of proprietors and possessors, this can be found in the gaps,
in all that which is not a continuation of their discourse, in the zero,
the O, the perfect circle that you invent to imprison them and to
overthrow them. [Pp. 112, 114]

Indeed few codes, from gestures to table manners, are un-
marked for sex.

Hence, a complete model for feminist criticism would account for the functioning of ideology in the encoding,
transmission, and decoding of messages, as well as the laws
governing the relationship of those messages to sociocultural
realities which are themselves codes subject to ideological uses.
Many semioticians have stated that ideology has a semiotic
function; few have dealt with how it functions.

Ideology functions at three different steps in the communication chain: at the moment of code creation; in the process of

textual production; and in the process of textual interpretation.[7] Taking woman to be a sign in both linguistic and nonlinguistic codes, we can see how ideology operates in each situation.

The significance of the sign "woman" in any given code is not congruent with the referent—real women. Out of the endless variety of features that may be observed in women, the culture selects only a few as relevant to a given code and invests those features with semiotic status. For instance, in American culture, the presence or absence of hair on the arms is not relevant to the perception of a given woman as "womanly" or "feminine," whereas the presence or absence of hair on the legs is invested with semiotic significance.

Since signs do not incorporate *all* features of the referent, there must exist an ideology, defined as a system of values that function as normative guidelines for the selection of relevant features. It is precisely in the encoding of features from the referent into signs that the general ideological stance of a culture makes itself felt. In a masculinist culture like our own, the cultural and linguistic encodings of biological sex into gender rules reflect an androcentric bias. Ideology, therefore, is transferred directly into the sets of relationships between signs that form semiotic systems and, ultimately, culture.

The writer must take these preexisting codes and use them to produce a text. If, as Eco argues, the literary text is a kind of idiolect,[8] then the function of the writer is to recombine linguistic signs to create new meanings. The ideological stance of the individual author enters the communication chain as the author selects signs and combines them to form a text. When we speak of the "unique world vision," or of the style of an author, we are referring to those points in the text where the author manipulates words to alter their relationships.[9] I would argue that all such manipulation reflects ideological value structures.

The author has essentially three choices in the selection of signs. She or he may choose to use signs in such a way that their accepted meaning is not altered at all, may use them and emphasize certain encoded features, or may alter the sign's meaning by adding or deleting features. In the first instance, the writer merely reaffirms the dominant ideology of the culture and lends it validity. In the second case, the writer, by emphasizing some features of the sign, may participate in the creation of stereotypes, which may be defined as a secondary overcoding of the sign which limits further its congruence to the referent. Research by Chabrol and Casalis on the discourse of popular magazines has shown that mass publications tend to emphasize only a limited number of features already encoded by the culture. Hence, *Penthouse*'s excessive devotion to secondary sex characteristics of females does not challenge the accepted encodings of femininity but reiterates constantly and ad nauseam two or three aspects of the significance given to the female body.[10]

The author may disagree with the dominant ideology and seek to correct its faults by altering the significance given to various signs. Using a variety of verbal techniques, the writer can recode the preexisting sign in a new way, changing its signification for the reader. Since both writers and readers participate in the assumption that words refer to "reality"—to the codes of the culture—verbal manipulation of signs may alter relationships between the presumed referents of the words. If verbal manipulation is carried too far, however, the text may become incomprehensible. The reader can accept alteration of the language only so long as enough of the original encoding remains to permit observation of both the original and the altered meaning.

Finally, ideology functions at the end of the communication chain. The reader's own ideological stance will determine the extent to which ideological values encoded into the text are perceived at all, and if perceived, whether they are accepted or rejected.[11] The process of reading is one of translating the linguistic sign into concepts that can also be applied to other cultural codes. Hence, the reader will view the formal linguistic and literary structures of the text as either congruent or noncongruent with the cultural structures that determine the reader's perception of reality. It is important to keep in mind that the organization of the dominant ideology is generally perceived as "true" or "natural," while competing ideologies are generally perceived as limited or "biased," if not as "false."[12] Textual structures that do not alter the encodings of the dominant ideology will pass unnoticed by most readers. The reader who accepts the dominant ideology will perceive the text as "realistic" or "true" to the extent that it reaffirms dominant social codes. If it deviates from them, the reader will lend credence to its message only to the degree that the text conforms to the reader's own ideological position. Hence, a reader who accepts as valid the negative encoding of women in a patriarchal society will reject an overtly feminist text as "distorted," while a feminist reader will not.

Ideology therefore functions as the set of principles by which a dominant group in a culture selects from the real world those features of referents it wishes to consider significant in its semiotic systems. This preexisting coding provides the shared raw material for textual production and textual decoding, which may be altered by the writer and reader at each end of the communication chain.

To illustrate some techniques an author may use in restructuring the ideological content of cultural signs, I want to examine a typical passage from *Les Guérillères*. I selected this work because Wittig, more than most writers, is conscious of the semiotic functions of complex signs like myths, rituals, and social systems. A brief allusion to such complex signs is sufficient to trigger an automatic set of assumptions on the part of a reader familiar with both the meaning of such signs and their function in cultural systems. In passages preceding the one below, Wittig has introduced the image of the circle as a sign representing all aspects of woman. She has also inserted into the text a number of sun goddess myths, which are part of the culture of the collective heroine referred to simply as "elles" (the women).

Dans la légende de Sophie Ménade, il est question d'un verger planté d'arbres de toutes les couleurs. Une femme nue y marche. Son beau corps est noir et brillant. Ses cheveux sont des serpents fins et mobiles qui produisent une musique à chacun de ses mouvements. C'est la chevelure conseillère. On l'appelle ainsi parce qu'elle communique par la bouche de ses cent mille serpents avec la femme porteuse de la chevelure. Orphée, le serpent préféré de la femme qui marche dans le jardin, sans cesse lui conseille de manger du fruit de l'arbre du milieu du jardin. La femme goute du fruit de chacun des arbres en demandant à Orphée le serpent comment reconnaître le bon. Il lui est répondu qu'il est étincelant, qu'à le regarder simplement on a la joie au coeur. Ou bien il lui est répondu que, dès qu'elle aura mangé le fruit, sa taille se developpera, elle grandira, ses pieds ne quitteront pas le sol tandis que son front touchera les étoiles. Et lui Orphée et les cent mille serpents de sa chevelure s'étendront de part et d'autre de son visage, ils lui feront une couronne brillante, ses yeux deviendront pales comme des lunes, elle aura la connaissance. Elles alors pressent Sophie Ménade de questions. Sophie Ménade dit que la femme du verger aura la vraie connaissance du mythe solaire que tous les

textes ont à dessein obscurci. Elles alors la pressent de questions.
Sophie Ménade dit, soleil qui épouvantes et ravis/insecte multico-
lore, chatoyant/tu te consumes dans la mémoire nocturne/sexe qui
flamboie/le cercle est ton symbole/de toute éternité tu es/de toute
éternité tu seras. Elles, à ces paroles, se mettent à danser, en frap-
pant la terre de leurs pieds. Elles commencent une danse circulaire,
en battant des mains, en faisant entendre un chant dont il ne sort
pas une phrase logique. [Pp. 72–73]

[Sophie Ménade's tale has to do with an orchard planted with trees
of every color. A naked woman walks therein. Her beautiful body is
black and shining. Her hair consists of slender mobile snakes which
produce music at her every movement. This is the hortative head of
hair. It is so called because it communicates by the mouths of its
hundred thousand snakes with the woman wearing the headdress.
Orpheus, the favourite snake of the woman who walks in the garden, keeps advising her to eat the fruit of the tree in the center of
the garden. The woman tastes the fruit of each asking Orpheus the
snake how to recognize that which is good. The answer given is that
it sparkles, that merely to look at it rejoices the heart. Or else the
answer is given that, as soon as she has eaten the fruit, she will
become taller, she will grow, her feet will not leave the ground
though her forehead will touch the stars. And he Orpheus and the
hundred thousand snakes of her headdress will extend from one
side of her face to the other, they will afford her a brilliant crown,
her eyes will become as pale as moons, she will acquire knowledge.
Then the women besiege Sophie Ménade with questions. Sophie
Ménade says that the woman of the orchard will have a clear understanding of the solar myth that all the texts have deliberately obscured. Then they besiege her with questions. Sophie Ménade says,
Sun that terrifies and delights/multicolored iridescent insect you
devour yourself in night's memory/blazing genital/the circle is
your symbol/you exist from all eternity/you will exist for all eter-
nity. At these words the women begin to dance, stamping the
ground with their feet. They begin a round dance, clapping their
hands, giving voice to a song from which no coherent phrase
emerges. [Pp. 52–53]

While the story, explictly labeled as legend, seems unfamiliar
to the female audience (they question the narrator about it), we,
as readers, immediately recognize this as a rewriting of the
Eden myth. The juxtaposition of a woman, a garden, a snake,
and fruit that gives knowledge evokes for the reader not only
the original Eden myth, but all subsequent uses and interpretations of it. The myth has, in effect, become a complex sign
signifying, in part, woman's weakness as the source of sin and
misery in the world. By alluding to the myth, Wittig relies on
the reader's knowledge of the ideological implications for
women of the Eden story.

Wittig evokes Eden only to strip it of certain key components and substitute others. In so doing, she simultaneously causes the reader to recognize the androcentric ideology of the original encoding, and creates a new, feminist version. Note that the referent here is not the "real world" or real women, but a preexisting cultural semiotic system of religious myth.

Expecting to find Eve in the garden, we are confronted with a nude black woman with hair of snakes. These elements suffice to call forth for the reader the myth of Medusa, a female figure presented as a powerful, life-threatening force. With this substitution, Wittig replaces the weak-willed Eve with a stronger image. Whereas in the original myth Medusa was a horrible monster, here she is characterized as beautiful.

A more direct substitution follows, when the favorite serpent is named Orpheus. The serpent in the garden is no longer an independent Satan tempting woman, but a subordinate counselor. This renaming results in a complex shift of ideological values that reverses the original myth. The snake as Orpheus is a musician leading woman out of a hell of ignorance, rather than a devil luring woman to a fall from grace.

While these two substitutions go far to recode the Eden myth, Wittig recognizes that the absence of an expected sign is also a sign. Both God and Adam are absent, a void the reader is sure to notice. The Eve figure here is no helpmate: there is no male present and no one to whom she could be subordinate. This elimination of man from the garden also eliminates those aspects of the Eden myth most used against women. Further, as there is no God whose power might be challenged by a human who acquired knowledge, the fruit is not forbidden, and the eating of it does not constitute a sin. On the contrary, upon eating the fruit, Eve-Medusa will herself become a goddess to replace the absent male God.

Finally, Wittig's narrator comments upon the relationship between this new Eden and the original. She says the texts have deliberately obscured the sun goddess myth, thereby accusing preceding texts of falsifying reality. The reader must supply the rest of the accusation: that male culture substituted a male deity and an androcentric ideology for an earlier female religion. Finally, the circle image is repeated in the poem and dance performed by the women.

With three simple techniques, in simple language, Wittig has substituted a positive feminist ideological marker for the negative masculinist marker of the Eden myth. We can see in this brief passage all three levels of the semiotic functioning of ideology. First, Wittig must deal with a preexisting system of religious myth—an encoding of reality shared by the reader. Second, she takes this raw material and, through manipulation of language, transforms the original semiotic significance of the myth from negative to positive with respect to women. Upon receiving the message, we, as readers, must compare this altered encoding with the original and, according to our own ideological perspectives, accept or reject it.[13]

If we accept the semiotic premise that human culture is a set of sign systems, then it seems to me that we must accept as a corollary that such systems are inherently ideological. I have outlined here the major ways in which ideology enters the literary text, but much research is needed to determine the processes by which ideological structures are encoded into language and the text, and how the reader's ideological system operates in the decoding and interpretation of texts. Ultimately, such a semiotic approach could resolve the question of the relationships between literary discourse and the sociohistorical context within which it is created.

1. Michael Riffaterre, *Semiotics of Poetry* (Bloomington: Indiana University Press, 1978), pp. 1–5.

2. Monique Wittig, *Les Guérillères* (Paris: Editions de Minuit, 1969). All citations from this work are from the English translation by David LeVay (New York: Avon, 1973).

3. See, for instance, the rejection for ideological reasons of structural and semiotic models made by the following critics: Françoise Gaillard, "Code(s) littéraire(s) et idéologie," *Littérature*, No. 12 (1973), pp. 21–35; Jacques Leenhardt, "Modèles littéraires et idéologie dominante," *Littérature*, No. 12, pp. 12–20; Fraya Katz-Stoker, "The Other Criticism: Feminism vs. Formalism," *Images of Women in Fiction: Feminist Perspectives*, ed. Susan Koppelman Cornillon (Bowling Green, Ohio: Bowling Green University Popular Press, 1973), pp. 315–27.

4. Monique Wittig, in a speech to the Modern Language Association, New York, December 1978.

5. Annette Kolodny, in her unpublished paper "Critical Models as Tools or Tribulations," Modern Language Association, New York, December 1978, concludes that semiotic models as constituted to date are unacceptable for feminist critics because they rely upon the assumption that "men and women share the same consensual reality or realities." This problem is still evident, even among semioticians interested in ideology.

Juri Lotman and his colleagues have done considerable research into the relations between literature and social context, but the models they propose are problematic for feminist criticism for the reason Kolodny points out. Lotman and A. M. Pjatigorskij, in "Le Texte et la fonction," *Semiotica* 1 (1969), state: "Du point de vue de l'étude de la culture, seuls existent les messages qui sont des textes. Les autres, en quelque sorte, n'existent pas et ne sont pas pris en considération par les chercheurs" (p. 209). Their ensuing discussion of the criteria for distinguishing, among messages, "texts" and "non-texts" reveals that only those works endowed by the dominant ideology with value and prestige count as "texts" worthy of semiotic attention. Works of art are in principle "texts," but Lotman and Pjatigorskij do not say who establishes the criteria for the "artistic" work (p. 211). As Cesare Segre has pointed out in "Culture and Modeling Systems," *Critical Inquiry* 4, no. 3 (1978):525–37, the Soviet semioticians' conception of "text" eliminates from the domain of cultural semiotics precisely those messages which challenge the dominant ideology. In literary terms, then, we would consider as "texts" worthy of attention only those works canonized by the dominant ideology.

It is obvious that, by the relegation to the limbo of "nontexts" works not validated by those in power, much women's writing would be excluded from the model: those works by women which did achieve "textual" status would be those which did not radically challenge the patriarchal order.

The Soviet semioticians, like their colleagues elsewhere, also assume the objectivity of semiotics itself—an assumption challenged by Julia Kristeva at a colloquium devoted to Soviet semiotics and published as "La Sémiologie comme science des idéologies," *Semiotica* 1 (1969):196–204. She distinguishes "la sémiotique," the empirical study of signs, from "la sémiologie," which analyzes ideology within the discourse of semiotics itself (p. 196). As a discourse, semiotics is grounded in a historical and cultural moment and is inherently ideological. This questioning of the objectivity of scientific discourse is also occurring among feminist scientists.

I would suggest that semiotics cannot attain real usefulness for literary criticism until this distinction becomes unnecessary: unless the "empirical science" is constantly aware of the ideological assumptions behind it, it cannot hope to describe accurately sign functions. It is this necessity inherent within the discipline that makes it a potential bridge between ideological and formalist criticisms.

6. Here again feminist theory comes into conflict with that of Lotman et al. One of their primary notions is that of "secondary modeling systems," including literature and art. They view language as a primary model, and artistic systems as formed by analogy with language. But feminists do not view language structures as value-free "forms": they are seen as tools of the dominant ideology. In the foreword to *Le Corps lesbien* (Paris: Editions de Minuit, 1973), Wittig explains that even the pronoun *je* is alienating for the feminist writer. From a feminist point of view, the Lotman theory of art merely enshrines patriarchal systems embedded in language without questioning their ideological functions. For an extensive study of linguistic and literary forms as tools of the dominant ideology, see Crowder, "Narrative Structures and the Semiotics of Sex in the Novels of Alain Robbe-Grillet," (Ph.D. diss., University of Wisconsin, 1977), in which I develop a feminist literary critical model based upon semiotics.

7. Ideology clearly intervenes also in a fourth instance: the actual transmission of the message. In the case of literature, as well as other types of discourse, the means of transmission are generally controlled by the dominant group. Access to the media is a privilege that can be used to censor messages threatening to the dominant ideology. The case of women's writing is exemplary: the history of women's literature shows that it has not been defined as "art" worth preserving; that women have experienced extreme difficulty getting their works into print, etc. Women writers, like others outside the dominant ideology, have frequently resorted to the traditional outlets of repressed

groups: "samizdat" style self-publishing, small alternative presses, the "private genres" (letters, diaries), and so on.

The question of ideological control of the media is another area where Lotman's and Pjatigorskij's definition of "text" makes their model unacceptable. They state that a "text," by virtue of its value, will be given access to the most developed media. In a literate society, for instance, a message would not be a "text" unless deemed worthy of publication. This same principle applies today to the electronic media ("Le Texte," pp. 206–7). The ideological censorship of messages from the media means that, once again, works not acceptable to the dominant culture would not be "texts" and hence would not be worthy of semiotic attention, according to Lotman and Pjatigorskij.

8. Umberto Eco, *A Theory of Semiotics* (Bloomington: Indiana University Press, 1976).

9. On this point, I agree with Riffaterre *(Semiotics of Poetry)* that the important parts of the text are those points where the reader notes an "ungrammaticality," but I would add that such points are not only linguistically, but semiotically, deviant.

10. Claude Chabrol, *Le Récit féminin* (The Hague: Mouton, 1971) examines the rhetoric and ideology of French women's magazines. Matthieu Casalis, "The Discourse of *Penthouse:* Rhetoric and Ideology," *Semiotica* 15, no. 4 (1975): 355–91, is a model study.

11. I believe most readers simply fail to perceive the ideological underpinnings of large portions of texts, because it never occurs to them to question the dominant ideology and its world view.

12. See Mary Ellmann, *Thinking about Women* (New York: Harvest Books, 1968), for a discussion of this phenomenon among literary critics.

13. See Roland Barthes, *Mythologies* (Paris: Editions du Seuil, 1957), part 2, "Le Mythe, aujourd'hui," for one semiotic approach to the use of mythic structures for ideological purposes.

Noman, Everywoman: Claudine Herrmann's *Les Voleuses de langue*

Carolyn A. Durham
College of Wooster

FOR a contemporary feminist critic, Claudine Herrmann bears surprisingly close ties to two earlier and male-dominated movements in France, the New Novel and New Criticism. Indeed, the significance of the cover page of her essay seems in perfect keeping with the practice of the former. Herrmann has selected a richly overdetermined title for her work: the linguistic economy of French requires a simultaneous reading of "les voleuses de langue" as those women who both *steal* language and make it *fly*. Coincidence would have it that Mme de Lafayette, one of Herrmann's earliest thieves of male language, grew up as Mlle de La Vergne, aptly recalling Laverna, Roman goddess of theft.[1] Herrmann does not point out to us the comparable wealth of her own name, but it proves as important as the title for advance notice of the text to come: Herr-man(n), twice male, doubly alienated in a virile culture. Nor is the third element of the cover design, "des femmes," any more gratuitous and innocent, for to publish with the "éditions des femmes" is to announce a particular feminist context, characterized most significantly by the conviction that women do or will speak a distinctly different language from men.[2]

Elaine Marks first introduced *Les Voleuses de langue* to an American public as feminist literary criticism: "one of the few texts that we might refer to as literary criticism within the *écriture féminine* inquiry."[3] Indeed, French feminists concerned with women's discourse[4] have proved far less interested than

their American counterparts in reading female literary texts of
the past or present, far more interested in developing a
theoretical foundation for the production of texts of the future.
Marks situates Herrmann in the camp of those French feminists who believe in a fundamental difference in the language
of men and women. Far more significant for an understanding
of Herrmann is the split Marks discovers within this group
itself:

> But there is an important cleavage within the upholders of differ-
> ence between those who criticize all theorizing, all abstract formula-
> tion as male (Duras, Herrmann, Rochefort, Gagnon, Leclerc) and
> those who are themselves theoreticians, who utilize male theories
> and move on to their own.[5]

Marks thus positions Herrmann on the side of those women
who reject all theories, and theory itself, as uniquely male.
While it quickly becomes clear that Herrmann criticizes all
theory as masculine—such is indeed one of the central concepts
of *Les Voleuses de langue*—she would appear to make a distinction between her critical principles and her practice. It is therefore tempting to place Herrmann on both sides of the issue at
one and the same time; to criticize theorizing as masculine does
not prevent her from using masculine theories as the foundation of her own criticism. Whether the latter is theoretical or
not is another question.

Since Roland Barthes defined criticism as a metalanguage,
we have known that a critical methodology can and should
offer itself to our appreciation independently of the works the
critic chooses to discuss. This proves particularly valid in the
case of Herrmann, who offers less insight into the particular
French texts she analyzes than into the current intellectual context of French feminism. This can already be seen in the central
title image of *Les Voleuses de langue*. Herrmann's understanding
of the term *vol*, always meaning at once "theft" and "flight," is
borrowed from Hélène Cixous, who has made it a key element
of women's discourse and of her own vocabulary:

> Flying is woman's gesture—flying in language and making it fly. We
> have all learned the art of flying and its numerous techniques; for
> centuries we've been able to possess anything only by flying; we've
> lived in flight, stealing away, finding, when desired, narrow pas-
> sageways, hidden crossovers. It's no accident that *voler* has a double
> meaning, that it plays on each of them and thus throws off the

agents of sense. It's no accident: women take after birds and robbers just as robbers take after women and birds. They *(illes)* go by,
fly the coop, take pleasure in jumbling the order of space, in disorienting it, in changing around the furniture, dislocating things
and values, breaking them all up, emptying structures, and turning
property upside down.[6]

It is my intention here to present the central concepts of *Les
Voleuses de langue* to an English-speaking audience, to place
Herrmann in a critical context that will allow us to perceive the
originality of her methodology, and to read her essay as the
practice of a theory, as an example of women's discourse as
Herrmann understands it.

Men and women have different languages and understand-
ings; they do not perceive ideas and feelings in the same way.
For Herrmann, this starting point is initially highly personal;
her essay grew out of the stupefaction she experienced upon
attempting to initiate herself into a virile knowledge and culture. To some extent, this is a modern feminist version of the
eighteenth-century principle of the naive narrator; because all
of culture is virile, women alone can perceive certain of its
characteristics hidden to men. But what is first presented as
feeling, as intuition—"it has often seemed to me that"—evolves
in the course of a sentence into "this fact . . . obvious for many"
(p. 5). Since feminism would seem to suppose for Herrmann a
consciousness of her difference as woman, it is entirely appropriate that she begin by making this assumption clear.
Moreover, within the course of her essay, Herrmann also attempts to illustrate how a female language might be structured,
thus offering her own text as the clearest evidence for her
position. In spite of this fact of difference, however, perceptible
to all women and perceived by many, Herrmann believes that
female liberation has to date taken a sterile and self-destructive
path: "the emancipation of women was developing in a single
direction: their access to the values on hand, in other words, to
virile values, without their particular ways of seeing, of feeling,
and of thinking ever being taken into consideration" (p. 5).[7] In
rejecting as unproductive the integration of women, Herrmann
reflects the "anti-feminist" position of the editors of the
"éditions des femmes" who have dismissed feminism as a reformist movement in which revolutionary change is abandoned
in favor of power within the current political and social system.[8] In an attempt to understand and value what is uniquely

female, Herrmann proposes to examine the question of difference from a variety of perspectives: to study literary, historical,
and legal texts "to show how culture is colonized" (p. 5).

Herrmann's critical methodology first appears as an absence
or a refusal of method, as the term is generally understood.
What she in fact rejects is the notion of system that, for Herrmann, is always masculine, always abstract, and always subjective; a system never reflects reality but only the longing for
order and unity characteristic of our own mental categories.
For Herrmann, the best critical *method,* since she nonetheless
uses the term, is to offer the reader a series of glimpses. Herrmann's only announced principle is the priority of the object
under study, of the text under analysis; any further definition
of her methodology can only be induced from her practice.

At first reading, the six chapters of *Les Voleuses de langue*
might easily be mistaken for a collection of essays. Although we
are in fact in the presence of a coherent sequence of ideas and
not of a series of independent articles, the evolution of Herrmann's thought is carefully nonsystematic; it is neither logical
nor causal nor linear. That we may ultimately appreciate the
unique manner in which Herrmann has structured her thought
in *Les Voleuses de langue,* it is necessary to begin with a rapid and
chronological presentation of her argument, with a glimpse of
her glimpses.

In her opening chapter, Herrmann founds her argument on
the principle so aptly reflected in her own name: women are
twice alienated. Since the present culture is entirely virile, the
woman who seeks access to knowledge is obliged to let "a little
man" grow within her (p. 8). Forced at the same time to live as a
female, she must conform in that role as well to a male
definition of *woman.* Necessarily schizophrenic or hermaph-
roditic, and effectively "defeminized," she greets with astonish-
ment the pronouncement that she is more "natural" than any
male. Men have always used the sex of language as their tool of
alienation, and from the primitive tribes studied by Lévi-
Strauss to the present women have been consistently punished
for their failure to understand the language denied to them.
Herrmann examines the situation of two precursors, Lady
Murasaki and Mme de Lafayette, in the title article of her second chapter. In their respective novels, *The Tale of Genji* and *La
Princesse de Clèves,* these early thieves of language adopted an
identical solution that allowed both of them to be heard and to

avoid alienation into virile values. Both use to two new ends the convention that permits a man to seduce several women: to draw attention to the suffering of women, to create the man of the future.

Herrmann next describes the "virile system" whose dominant abstraction is revealed through systematic and hierarchical structures. To show us that male reasoning is always identical, Herrmann compares surrealism with the judicial system. The conclusion is that man sees only himself everywhere and annihilates everywhere what is outside of himself, notably woman:

> every man has a tendency to organize the world—whether we are dealing with a head of state, a thinker, or even a poet—according to a system of which he is the center and which has as its goal the maximum destruction of other existing systems.
> Our world is thus bristling with a phallic ensemble of bizarre constructions. [P. 64]

Herrmann goes on to examine two of these constructions, love and madness. Women's consistent dissatisfaction with male love has led to female madness as men have both defined and provoked it. Woman is always either hysterical—she who does not dare to express herself—or delirious—she who does express herself, who has the audacity to believe that her dreams can be realized.

Herrmann next argues for a feminist criticism, using two examples from different disciplines to illustrate her technique. From literary history, she selects a novella of Barbey d'Aurevilly's, "At a Dinner of Atheists," which she reads as a reflection of male misogyny and fundamental homosexuality. From Roman history, Herrmann analyzes the epoch that includes the rape of Lucretia, the death of Virginia, and the feminist activity of the Bacchantes. Although the mistreatment of women led in every case to an apparent liberalization of Roman law, the consequence in fact was the ever-increasing repression of women.

In her final chapter, Herrmann examines male and female conceptions of time and of space. Both temporal and spatial coordinates prove hostile to women. Space is inherently masculine as the domain of system and hierarchy, of domination and conquest, of limitation and rejection; and women, thus excluded from space, react with hate and denial. Time proves still more threatening as it robs women of childhood, their only moment of freedom, and destroys physical beauty, their only claim to male love. In reaction, women choose to live in the present to protect the affective values they hold most dear.

In the attempt to place Herrmann's thought in the critical context that I believe to be hers, my purpose is obviously not to denigrate her work but rather to determine her originality and, more importantly, her difference as woman. Herrmann belongs to French New Criticism, to that movement which, beginning with Bachelard, attempted to renew French university criticism. In a general context, New Criticism includes much of Barthes, who was principally responsible for the theoretical coherence of the group, those critics who have taken various thematic approaches—Poulet, Richard, Starobinsky—and those critics who have attempted to adapt a social science methodology to the study of literary texts: Mauron with psychoanalysis, Goldmann with Marxist sociology, Sartre and Doubrovsky with philosophy.[9] Although we are dealing with a uniquely male movement with which Herrmann recognizes no direct parentage, she would seem to share certain of their basic premises. Other feminists who are exploring the question of language in France are drawing heavily upon the work of Derrida in philosophy and Lacan in psychoanalysis,[10] and it would be surprising if no woman were to benefit from the wealth of New Criticism as well. And although the movement no longer deserves the epithet "new," it does represent the most recent development in what can still be called literary criticism in France.

Like the New Critics, Herrmann practices an immanent criticism whose object is the work under study. Yet in spite of their belief in immanence, the New Critics all tend to insert the work into the system of their choice; each deviates from an originally limited point of view until this latter succeeds in englobing all aspects of the work under study.[11] The practice is so consistent that it is difficult not to read Herrmann's insistence that she attempts "a critical path which identifies with its object without drawing it into a system" as a direct attack on her male precursors (pp. 60–61). In both cases, the respect of immanence is a direct reflection of a world view determined by sex, and Herrmann's refusal to let her own thought patterns take precedence over objective reality implicitly defines her methodology as feminist:

Man so prefers himself to what surrounds him that he places his mental categories ahead of those of objective reality. . . .

From this initial act proceeds a vision of the world, precisely the one which distinguishes the man from the woman.

The woman, indeed, always obliged to take others into account as well as a material reality from which she escapes less easily than the man, can only imagine a cosmos of which she is not the center. [P. 50]

Herrmann also shares with the New Critics the principle of polyvalence, which insists on a plurality of readings and of meanings for any text. *Les Voleuses de langue* is an intentionally open-ended work; Herrmann presents it as no more than a trial attempt and she appeals to her readers to continue her efforts in other areas, as varied as possible. As early as her introduction, Herrmann acknowledges that another choice of texts would undoubtedly have produced different conclusions, as would the work of other critics on the same texts. Such a fact is not of a nature to disturb Herrmann, however, who states clearly her belief in the coexistence of contradictory truths: "Life is full of contradictions, as is thought, and science itself is far from being exempt from them" (p. 6). Herrmann thus places herself in the critical context of Roland Barthes, who distinguishes carefully between validity and truth; literary criticism is concerned only with the former:

> For if criticism is only a metalanguage, that means that its task is in no way the discovery of "truths," but only of "validities." In and of itself, a language is not true or false, it is valid or it isn't: valid, in other words, constituting a coherent system of signs.[12]

But where Barthes brings us back again to the concept of system, temporarily if not inherently limiting, Herrmann is always mindful of the necessity of polyvalence or of what Doubrovsky characterizes as "oversignification."[13] To the surprise, no doubt, of many readers of Simone Weil, Herrmann discovers a female conception of space in the work of this writer "entirely alienated by her formation in virile culture" (p. 140), but such a reading can never be exhaustive:

> These observations are not at all intended, however, to reduce the work of Simone Weil to signifieds relative to her condition. They do not exclude other interpretations. Works are like dreams; they can

have several meanings. We have no wish here to reduce any work to
a single meaning. [P. 140]

Nonetheless, Herrmann also accepts with New French Criticism the principle of an ideological orientation. The fact of
accepting a plurality of readings does not prevent the critic
from preferring a particular interpretation that he or she has
announced. It is in fact essential that the critic choose at least a
point of view, if not an ideology. That which Herrmann selects,
for we are dealing here with the former, has the particular
merit of supporting the preceding principle of polyvalence:

> feminist criticism consists of posing the point of view of the
> woman—not by the exclusion of other data, which would lead to a
> falsified and necessarily partial result—but at all times and in all
> places, in such a way that this question is not *erased* but *integrated*
> into the totality of elements which permit us to proceed to an analy-
> sis. [P. 123]

Among the New Critics, Herrmann would seem to be most
clearly allied with Georges Poulet, particularly in the final chapter of *Les Voleuses de langue* where she also selects the categories
of time and space as the axes of her criticism. But, in fact, their
resemblance is limited to this very general choice of an initially
similar focus. For Poulet, as for the other New Critics, the literary work always remains the expression of an individual. He
does not therefore question the "l'homme et l'oeuvre" relationship that has always been fundamental to French university
criticism. Herrmann is already at fault, by definition, since were
she to remain within the traditional psychological domain, only
the relationship between the *woman* and the work could interest
her. And, in fact, Herrmann is far more interested in women as
a sexual classification than as individuals. It is explicit in Herrmann's reasoning that any female work viewed as the *expression*
of a life or of a social situation will necessarily reflect virile
values and be the product of alienation. Although Herrmann's
vocabulary reveals some confusion between *la femme,* women as
abstract entity, and *les femmes,* women as individuals, her preference for the former in no way results in an insensitiveness to
the specificity of a particular text. If, for example, Herrmann
argues for a female conception of space, she also demonstrates
how this conception is translated differently in the works of
individual women writers.

To establish a parallel between the last chapter of *Les Voleuses de langue* and Poulet's *Le Point de départ* appears almost essential. In the second volume of *Les Études sur le temps humain*, Poulet reads the experience of the instant, of the present moment, as the dominant temporality of the twentieth century; for Herrmann, this same experience characterizes the female conception of time. But whereas in Herrmann's work this female experience is valued in and of itself (without being either inferior or superior to the male experience, since Herrmann rejects all hierarchical systems), Poulet makes constant value judgments that stem from an a priori assumption which is at best questionable: the inferiority of the instant. For Poulet, the instant is always lived as a lack, as the nostalgia of duration and continuity.[14] How interesting, nonetheless, that the temporal experience which Poulet devalues should be precisely the one Herrmann defines as female. And it is surely significant that in the only chapter devoted to a woman author in the entire three volumes of his study on human time, Poulet associates the inadequacy of instantaneousness with Mme de Lafayette: "The central subject of *La Princesse de Clèves* is already sketched: how to establish or re-establish a continuity in existence amid the anarchic and destructive irruption, the radical discontinuity which is the very essence of passion."[15] Thus, Poulet arrives at the explanation and the importance of Mme de Clèves's confession to her husband, the famous *aveu:*

> Ah! to be able to rediscover in this way, were it by a blind obedience, were it at the price of another form of slavery, that continuity of self, that fidelity to self, which makes of life, not a chaos of instants, but a temporal unity![16]

Note Herrmann's contrasting value system:

> Male time is in fact only another system, the most redoubtable of all, the one which deprives you of the present in the name of the future, and which indefinitely adjourns the instant by crushing it under the past and the future.
> As soon as a woman expresses herself, it is generally to assert her right to the present moment, to affirm her refusal of a life alienated into social time so hostile to interior time. [Pp. 154–55]

Herrmann's critical orientation holds promise for those feminists who remain interested in the study of literary works. It is important to note that Herrmann offers us a reading of par-

ticular texts far more than a methodology of reading. Like
Starobinsky before her, one might even say that she simply
does rather interesting *explications de textes*. And the dangers are
the same: Herrmann's analysis at times comes precariously
close to pure tautology. That Herrmann should refuse to out-
line a method in detail is appropriate, of course, since she rejects all systematic thought as masculine. Herrmann seeks
above all to identify herself with the object under study; she is
therefore eclectic by definition and by choice. But her empirical
eclecticism has special significance in a feminist context where it
is particularly important that criticism avoid the tendency to
become prescriptive, to establish norms for how women ought
to write and read. Such has for too long been the practice of
men:

> The normative tone is admirable here: a woman "should." . . . Who
> decides for her? Stendhal, obviously. No one explains better than
> an enlightened man how necessary it is to be able to scorn a woman
> and by what means criticism bears on her person rather than on her
> words. [P. 33]

But because Herrmann's readings are nonetheless oriented,
they can provide a direction for future research, as she herself
would wish. One might ask, for example, whether or not the
coded procedure that she identifies in the novels of Lady
Murasaki and Mme de Lafayette is also to be found in the work
of other female precursors. The same question can be raised, in
general, for the conceptions of time and space Herrmann has
discovered in particular women's writings.

Herrmann has realized with the New Critics in general that
revolutionary thought is no doubt necessary to reawaken criticism. What others have done through Marxism, psychoanalysis,
and linguistics, Herrmann seeks to do through feminism. The
critical act is for Herrmann an affirmation of values, and her
tone is in no way objective or neutral. A few examples should
suffice: "This is what allows Rousseau to write absurdities such
as this" (p. 21); "We should not be surprised that such an immense absurdity is rarely commented upon" (p. 57); ". . . this
pitiful virile world . . ." (p. 65). Nonetheless, Herrmann has
managed to avoid certain limitations that other French feminists have willingly chosen to impose upon themselves. Herrmann speaks from a point of view that permits her to read texts
written by men as well as by women. Moreover, Herrmann does

succeed in reading female texts of the past and present without being content to simply call for a women's discourse of the future. Of particularly high value is the general accessibility of Herrmann's work; the greatest danger currently facing feminist criticism in France may well be the risk that it will or already has become so specialized and intellectualist as to prove incomprehensible, and therefore marginal and dismissible, to the great majority of French women. Most important of all, Herrmann never forgets that a written work is above all and before all a product of language.

Indeed, the failing of many new French critics, and of certain feminist critics as well, has been to ignore the literary text as a creation of language. Criticism, even "new," has had a tendency to dissociate the signifier from the signified, in order to grant privileged status to the latter. The problem is particularly severe for a movement in which the central issue in recent years has been to find and use an appropriate female language. As Carolyn Burke so aptly points out: "Regrettably, saying that women should see their sexual difference as a source of strength and write from their bodies does not always make this happen: much discussion of women's writing talks about the subject without managing to exemplify it."[17] Herrmann's considerable merit comes from her success in illustrating the female language of which she speaks, in demonstrating the process by which women can break free of male language.

On the level of the signified, Herrmann's work is a text about the theft of language. Far more interesting is the fact that on the level of the signifier, we see a theft of language in operation; Herrmann is herself the original thief of language. Moreover, Herrmann makes no effort to conceal this fact. Her text is stolen everywhere from men (from women as well but far less frequently) and the theft is obvious. Quotation is Herrmann's favorite procedure for incorporating a stolen discourse into her own. At one point, she quotes eleven straight pages from a novella by Barbey d'Aurevilly; if the fact is worth mentioning, it is because at least one third of Herrmann's book is quoted from others. She cites eighty authors, of whom fifty-three are men, and she quotes from some of them on numerous occasions. Having once quoted, Herrmann immediately intervenes anew to interpret, to analyze, to deconstruct male language; thus she is always acting on the double meaning of *voler*, to seize and to fly away. Herrmann's quotations from women permit her to establish a collective voice, an interesting contrast to the confusion of voice characteristic of many new French critics, and related to the experiments of other contemporary feminists, notably Monique Wittig in *Les Guérillères* and Luce Irigaray in *Ce Sexe qui n'en est pas un*. The anonymity and the plurality of the discourse are also reflected in the "voleuses" of the title.

The very movement of most chapters leads, via the organization of the quotations, from men to women; we therefore have a consistent motion away from and out of masculine culture. If one needs to specify "most chapters," it is because women, with the exception of Herrmann, are entirely absent from a discussion such as that of "The Virile System"; we are in the presence of a structure that is foreign to women and in which they are foreigners.

Since Herrmann's thesis is that the phenomenon that language and culture are always of masculine sex is the same in almost all societies, she quotes indiscriminately. She does not favor any epoch, reaching back to the Roman Empire and even touching primitive man through her reading of Lévi-Strauss, nor any civilization—hence a certain number of Oriental texts. There may be hidden thefts at work as well that operate particularly through Herrmann's unacknowledged ties to New French Criticism. She quotes only, but significantly, from Genette and Bachelard, from Genette to borrow a technical term (to steal language), from Bachelard to apply his thought to women's revery (to make language fly; pp. 141, 75).

One of Herrmann's central concerns in *Les Voleuses de langue* is female and male language, or, rather, the linguistic and rhetorical behavior of the two sexes. Women, whose thought processes are antisystematic or nonsystematic, suffer from aphasia of contiguity, from agrammatism; they have lost the ability to link words syntactically. The Greek etymology of the term proves of particular interest, given the status of women as a colonized people: *agrammatos,* in other words, "illiterate." In aphasia of contiguity, the grammatical function that remains in operation the longest is agreement, which maintains at least a trace of the harmony that, according to Herrmann, is dear to women. Herrmann's parallel understanding of the rhetorical functioning of male and female language characterizes men as essentially metonymical, women as essentially metaphorical:

"While intelligence can shine with all the fires—tiring at times, it is true—of metonymy, and add still other figures of speech to enhance its discourse, love has no choice: it can only transmit its essence—which is harmony—by metaphor" (p. 70).[18] Much has been written in recent years concerning the difference between metonymy and metaphor, some of which may eventually prove to relate to feminist theory developed along the lines of *Les Voleuses de langue*. But, for the moment, it seems for Herrmann to be simply a question of two entirely distinct and separate domains of which one, the male domain of metonymy, is characterized by syntax, contiguity, and hierarchy, and of which the other, the female domain of metaphor, is characterized by analogy, resemblance, and harmony.

It is this grammar, this male-female rhetoric, that provides the key to Herrmann's critical methodology, which explains the articulation of her thought in *Les Voleuses de langue*. Herrmann proceeds not only by the quotation of texts but also by the constant linking of two or more texts. The key words of her critical vocabulary are "to compare," "to bring together or unite" *(rapprocher)*, and "analogy." Aside from the linkings that Herrmann immediately establishes for her readers, the essay contains a consistent pattern of other parallels which they must recognize for themselves. As in much of the New Novel, Herrmann's text is woven with a network of relationships, of passages, of motifs, and of themes that call and recall each other. For example, Herrmann analyzes within a text of Breton's a dissimulated portrait of women of which the principal elements—a letter, a seal, the absence of an address—are also an integral part of Barbey d'Aurevilly's novella, discussed much later (pp. 62–63, 116). Elsewhere, it is a question of the repetition of key concepts in ever-changing contexts—the woman who is at one and the same time garrulous and mute, the woman who confuses the literal and the figurative, the alienation of women in a virile world, the dichotomy between justice and law, the rejection by women of systems, and so on. To examine a single example in detail, Herrmann introduces the concept of the confusion of meaning early in her opening chapter. Claude Lévi-Strauss has discovered in his study of American Indians that "the woman can in particular be guilty of two faults: the first consists of taking the figurative for the literal and the second of taking the literal for the figurative" (p. 12).

The rebel Zelda Fitzgerald announces the modern feminist by accepting the linguistic flaw of her sex and using it as a weapon against an oppressive system:

> Zelda Fitzgerald calls the firemen in the middle of the night:
> —Where is the fire? asks the chief.
> —Here, says Zelda, pointing to her lower abdomen.
> By this dazzling ellipsis which, *by voluntarily confusing the literal and the figurative* . . . , assumes the linguistic destiny of the woman, Zelda rejects both the education of the honorable man [*l'honnête homme*] (which requires that firemen not be disturbed without reason) and that of the honorable woman, which requires that she keep silent about her physical desires. [P. 26, emphasis mine]

Lady Murasaki's young heroine, although she is the living incarnation of love and poetry, cannot comprehend her lover's verbal expression of these: "she therefore hastens to confuse the literal and the figurative, to take the figurative for the literal" (p. 45). Herrmann herself is not entirely free from the flaw: "But perhaps it is only a question here of Breton's wit and to take it seriously may amount to confusing the literal with the figurative myself" (p. 60); this is not surprising, given its pervasiveness: "the confusion of the literal and the figurative, in other words what connotes femininity itself" (p. 84). To the extent that metaphor consists of a transfer of meaning—the use of a concrete term, for example, in a figurative context—Herrmann has identified a female rhetoric in which the traditional flaw is transposed into a value.

Although one might argue that such thematic repetition is inevitable given Herrmann's central concern with the linguistic repression of women, *Les Voleuses de langue* is in fact designed to offer the female equivalent of male cultural structure, even while making the assumptions of the latter explicit. Herrmann's text is an alternative response to the prevailing network announced in its first sentence:

> The woman who seeks to understand her condition finds herself immediately at grips with a totality of concepts both ambiguous and well-organized, a skillful network which pervades all cultural data, of which each link depends on the next and whose totality inevitably refers back to a male observer for whom the notion of woman, although subject to different phantasms, has been classified once and for all and has received a place which cannot be reexamined anymore than it can profoundly affect other questions. [P. 7]

The different subjects Herrmann treats are therefore superimposed by their structure; parallel but distinctive formal patterns characterize all aspects of male and female thought and behavior:

	Female	*Male*
Grammar:	agrammatism	syntax
Rhetoric:	metaphor	metonymy
Geography:	isolation	contiguity
Temporality:	instant	continuity
Affectivity:	love	intelligence
	(other-oriented)	(self-centered)

In every case, the man reaffirms his commitment to system and hierarchy, consistently assuming his place in the center or at the top; in every case, the woman rejects the male world, affirming her belief in the value of things and people in and among themselves, related to but separate from herself.

The structuring of Herrmann's text reflects a female architecture in other ways as well. Ideas and chapters are often linked by analogy rather than logical causality. For example, the first chapter, which includes allusions to several female precursors—Mme de Lafayette, Ninon de Lenclos, Zelda Fitzgerald—leads into a second chapter on the first thieves of language, among whom figures Mme de Lafayette. The third chapter, on the topic of the surrealist system and particularly Breton, calls necessarily to mind his *Amour fou* (Mad Love); this allusion produces a fourth chapter entitled "Amour et folie" (Love and Madness), even though its content bears no further relation to surrealism. The observation that Immalie, one of Mathurin's female characters, loves nature, introduces a preecological text of Virginia Woolf's, followed by a less perceptive but scientific male plea for ecological concern.

The text then points to itself everywhere, on the level of the signifier, as female writing as Herrmann is in the process of defining it on the level of the signified. It is therefore not surprising that *Les Voleuses de langue*, like many New Novels, should include a certain number of interior duplications. Herrmann often speaks of her own essay under the guise of describing the texts of others. For example, Herrmann characterizes Virginia Woolf's fictional world as radically feminine, and what she says of *The Waves* applies equally well to *Les Voleuses de*

langue: "We rediscover here the energetic refusal of all contiguity, and the book is, from the point of view of the signifiers as
from that of the signifieds, entirely founded on analogy which
gives it this poetic allure so rare in the novel" (p. 160). And even
rarer in literary criticism! Elsewhere, Herrmann speaks of
Woolf's effect on men:

> It is because the world which she creates is radically incommensur-
> able with that of men. It is impossible to find therein any basis for a
> comparison. The universe of men leaves her work in the same state
> as a term which has been treated by metaphor. It is no longer the
> same. It has made a cosmic voyage in language which has
> transformed it. [P. 158]

Herrmann, who literally treats the masculine universe as one of
the terms of a metaphor, also alters its status; she renders visible the sexual repressiveness of male language. In more general terms, Herrmann at one point distinguishes female love
from male intelligence:

> Love—which is not very strong in dialectics—cannot defend itself.
> It knows, however, that it perceives other relationships, just as sub-
> tle and ingenious, but impossible to demonstrate. . . . The relation-
> ships which it perceives are those of harmony or of discordance.
> [Pp. 68–69]

The relationships at play in the textual comparisons of *Les
Voleuses de langue* are precisely those of harmony—all
male/male or female/female analogies—or of discordance—all
male/female analogies.

Herrmann's analogical system also has the merit of reflecting
and supporting the female conceptions of time and space. Since
all concepts are superimposed by means of recall, allusion,
comparison, and analogy, there is no continuity and the text is
static, always present, always timeless. Yet, at the same time,
relationships established without concern for historical or social
contiguity produce a female space of harmonious unity outside
of any geographical context. Herrmann, moreover, is perfectly
conscious of the insolence of her analogical procedure; she
signals to us early in the process as she prepares to compare the
legal system to surrealism: "It seems at first sight that nothing
could be more dissimilar from the system of law than the surrealist system. *Only a woman can think to compare them*" (p. 52,
emphasis mine).

In the course of examining the ways in which female thought and language differ from the male norm, Herrmann may to some extent reinforce traditional stereotypes of women, especially by her emphasis on affective values. Yet, although Herrmann remains convinced that women and men are of an essentially different nature, she is also conscious of cultural influence and evolution. She is particularly successful in her suggestive illustration of a culture that has consistently repressed and sacrificed important values associated with women, whether or not these are solely and uniquely female. Herrmann's personal conception of female language as alogical, nonlinear, and nonchronological no doubt represents the general tendency of the twentieth century and, in this context, her ties to the New Novel and to New Criticism are particularly revealing. Nonetheless, the linguistic structuring of Herrmann's own essay, as well as that of the male and female texts from which she quotes, offers concrete evidence for the position she argues. Herrmann feels no need to reject any useful tool or insight, regardless of the sex of its originator, nor does she seek to be exclusive or prescriptive in her thinking. To the extent that feminism is an authentically interdisciplinary reexamination of cultural and sexual assumptions, founded upon a new egalitarianism, Herrmann's methodology offers a model from which feminists, both French and American, can successfully learn.

1. Claudine Herrmann, *Les Voleuses de langue* (Paris: éditions des femmes, 1976), p. 34. All subsequent page references are to this edition.

2. The publishing house "des femmes" was founded in 1974 by the Politics and Psychoanalysis group of the MLF (Mouvement de la libération de la femme). These women have always been particularly concerned with the problematics of women's writing. See Carolyn Greenstein Burke's discussion in "Report from Paris: Women's Writing and the Women's Movement," *Signs: Journal of Women in Culture and Society* 3 (1978):843–55.

3. Elaine Marks, "Women and Literature in France," *Signs* 3 (1978):839, n. 32.

4. Given the stereotypical connotations of "feminine" in English, it seems preferable to replace "feminine writing" *(écriture féminine)* with "women's writing" or "women's discourse."

5. Marks, "Women and Literature," p. 840. Among the latter, the most prominent are Hélène Cixous and Luce Irigaray.

6. Hélène Cixous, "The Laugh of the Medusa," trans. Keith Cohen and Paula Cohen, *Signs* 1 (1976):887. As the translators indicate, *illes* is a fusion of the masculine pronoun *ils,* which refers back to birds and robbers, with the feminine pronoun *elles,* which refers to women.

7. All translations from Herrmann are mine.

8. See Burke, "Report from Paris," p. 846.

9. See Serge Doubrovsky, *The New Criticism in France*, trans. Derek Coltman (Chicago: University of Chicago Press, 1973) and Laurent Lesage, *The French New Criticism: An Introduction and a Sampler* (University Park: Pennsylvania State University Press, 1967) for the best general discussion in English of the movement.

10. Lacan's appeal for feminists has always seemed surprising, given his close ties to Freudian psychoanalysis; it is clearly not shared by Herrmann. See *Les Voleuses*, pp. 81–83.

11. Thus Richard can create a "happy" Mallarmé *(L'Univers imaginaire de Mallarmé)* and Goldmann can make Junie the central character of *Britannicus (Le Dieu caché)*.

12. Roland Barthes, "Qu'est-ce que la critique," *Essais critiques* (Paris: Seuil, 1964), p. 255. My translation.

13. Doubrovsky, *The New Criticism*, p. 146.

14. Georges Poulet, *Le Point de départ* (Paris: Plon, 1964), see pp. 24–25, 27, 37.

15. Georges Poulet, *Études sur le temps humain* (Paris: Plon, 1950), p. 126. My translation.

16. Poulet, *Études*, p. 128. My translation.

17. Burke, "Report from Paris," p. 853.

18. Herrmann has previously associated intelligence with the male, love with the female.